Y0-AGJ-139

THE

F

WORD

THE
F
WORD

~

A Fiancée SHARES Her Story, from "I WILL" to "I DO"

Kelly Bare

CITADEL PRESS
Kensington Publishing Corp.
www.kensingtonbooks.com

CITADEL PRESS BOOKS are published by

Kensington Publishing Corp.
850 Third Avenue
New York, NY 10022

Copyright © 2007 Kelly Bare

All rights reserved. No part of this book may be reproduced in any form or by any means without the prior written consent of the publisher, excepting brief quotes used in reviews.

All Kensington titles, imprints, and distributed lines are available at special quantity discounts for bulk purchases for sales promotions, premiums, fund-raising, educational, or institutional use. Special book excerpts or customized printings can also be created to fit specific needs. For details, write or phone the office of the Kensington special sales manager: Kensington Publishing Corp., 850 Third Avenue, New York, NY 10022, attn: Special Sales Department; phone: 1-800-221-2647.

CITADEL PRESS and the Citadel logo are Reg. U.S. Pat. & TM Off.

First printing: February 2007

10 9 8 7 6 5 4 3 2 1

Printed in the United States of America

Library of Congress Control Number: 2006934741

ISBN-13: 978-0-8065-2805-2
ISBN-10: 0-8065-2805-2

For Jonathan

I often wonder when the wedding couple will realize just how much hard work they've taken on by consecrating that quirky emotion called love into the formal tie of marriage.

—Lois Smith Brady, "Vows" columnist, *The New York Times*

Contents

CONTENTS

Author's Note

THIS IS A BOOK ABOUT what it feels like to get married, written from a unique perspective: Because I was an editor at a relationship magazine, thinking about this stuff was my full-time job, as well as what I came home to at night, and I had access to all kinds of resources that most brides don't.

You could say it was the perfect wedding storm.

You'll notice that it is mostly about me, me, me; it's really memoir as advice. But to quote Henry David Thoreau, in his introduction to *Walden*, "I should not talk so much about myself if there were anybody else whom I knew as well."

It is not a tell-all, though. I'm sure it would help sales to call it that—*The F Word: A Fiancée Tells All!*—but I believe in truth in advertising. And I'm nowhere near ready to dish about everything that happened, or went through my head, when I was engaged. Instead, I give you almost everything that was within my comprehension at the time, and most things I was able to put into perspective shortly after the wedding. (It will take years to process all of it, I'm sure.)

I can't promise that every chapter will resonate with you.

And you surely will have, or have had, experiences outside the scope of this book. But if it has you nodding your head in recognition here and there, and feeling a bit less isolated, I'm happy. I had more moments of feeling completely overwhelmed and inadequate while I was engaged than during any other period of my life, and it always seemed like other brides were more levelheaded and serene than I. If I can prevent even one woman from feeling as I did, this book has done its job.

I learned that being a fiancée is a singular moment. It's a favored status; life lived at a slightly higher pitch. And it comes with a lot more responsibilities, heartache, and pressure than most people acknowledge. There's pressure to get engaged in the first place. There's pressure to plan a "perfect" wedding— which, by the way, doesn't exist—and there's pressure to look, and feel, perfect in the process.

But we've been set up to fail. You, my pretty bride-to-be, have a bull's-eye on your forehead. A multibillion-dollar industry has you in their sights, and just at a time when you're at your most vulnerable: going through a seismic identity shift, dealing with decades' worth of hopes and dreams centered on one day, trying to accommodate other people's (your fiancé's, your family's, his family's) identity shifts and hopes and dreams, and undertaking what likely will be the biggest planning project of your life. *All at the same time.*

Another thing I learned is that a lot of the traditional bridal flurry is misdirected. While the wedding can seem like the endgame, it's better for the two of you, and your relationship, to look at it as a momentary, though special, stop on the journey that began the moment you said "I will," and will continue long after that.

So now that you're engaged, sure, dive into the planning. Go visit reception venues. Try on a few dresses. Get in the tub with a glass of wine and a stack of wedding magazines, and savor them. But bring this book along, too. Think of it as a palate cleanser, which dares to go where advertising-supported women's magazines, intent on preserving the glossy myth of the happiest, most romantic time of your life, often fear to tread. Also consider it a safety zone, where you may obsess over the smallest detail of your engagement, wedding, or marriage-to-be in the quiet company of someone else who's been there.

Very early in our engagement, our friend Lauren hesitated when introducing me to someone as "Jonathan's fiancée." "I'm not sure how you feel about that word," she said. She was right to be cautious: At the time, I was very ambivalent about the F word. Slowly, though, I warmed up to it. I picked many fights with our wedding-obsessed culture—but I chose my battles carefully. And there were many times, far more than I expected at the outset, when I wouldn't have dreamed of resisting tradition.

Ultimately, I've come to think of this book as the story of (in a nod to Dr. Strangelove) "how I stopped worrying and learned to love my wedding."

I hope you love yours, too.

THE

F

WORD

June 1

POP GOES THE QUESTION

"Will you marry me?" is the first of many.

SOMETHING ASTONISHING HAPPENED to me this spring. My boyfriend of just-over-a-year asked me to marry him. Out of the blue, on a rainy, drowsy Saturday morning, as I lay staring at the back of his sleeping head, thinking how lucky I was to have him right there next to me, Jonathan rolled over, yawned, and started talking. He told me how happy he was, how lucky he felt to have *me* near *him* that morning, and every morning. I nodded along, making encouraging noises, but I had no inkling of what was about to happen, because I was distracted by the echo inside my own head . . . *me too, me too, me too*. And then suddenly he was pulling something out of the pocket of some pants hanging on a hook near the bed.

I don't remember much of what we said to each other, other than that my words—something like "of course, of course"—came through smiling tears, and he cried, too, and we laughed a lot, and it was a beautiful jumble. I later described the moment of proposal and acceptance to friends as the most purely positive, purely emotional reaction of my entire life—there have been plenty of times when I've gone primal, but never, ever before

that moment had sheer joy pulled the trigger. I guess nothing else in life has made such effortless sense.

Are you sitting there making little "gag me" motions with your finger? Seriously, you can admit it. No offense taken. It's a little sickening to me, even, to read it all spelled out like that. But every word of it is true, especially the mushy parts.

And that's what's so astonishing.

You see, not all that long ago, I would have told you that there was no "me" in "marriage." I couldn't see it happening; I didn't think I'd be pleased if it did.

But that was Before Jonathan.

Though I was *taken by surprise* in the moment of the proposal, I wasn't really *surprised*, if you buy that distinction. The bigger shocker was what had been happening gradually in my own head. A few months into our relationship, I already had a notion of where I wanted this thing to go; not too long after that, when the lights in his direction looked pretty green, I began cautiously mapping my trip. He made his move right around the time when I was beginning to strain to see if the signs I was looking for might be up ahead—and to wonder what the hell was happening to me.

The change had everything to do with him, and nothing to do with the desire to be married. Him I know, him I understand, him I love. He makes sense. But I have only the faintest glimmer of what marriage might really be about.

It's confounding. First off, how do I find harmony between my "issues" with marriage—which predate any personal experience with the subject—and my thoughts and feelings now that I have some skin in the game? "Don't let your politics get in the way," advised my boss, with whom I'm very close. "Just enjoy this." It's good advice, but hard to follow. For example, there's a part of me that thinks a woman's wait for a man's proposal is archaic and patriarchal and utter crap—but I honestly can't conjure an image of the me who would propose to a man, and I wouldn't trade our story for anything. I get indignant that a potential groom of a twenty-eight-year-old woman would think that her father had any say at all in whether she should get married—but at the same time, I was thrilled when Jonathan told me he'd consulted my family. My conscience smarts when I think about all the money and energy and long-lead-time planning it takes to pull off a wedding when there are so many other causes more worthy of those resources, but occasionally I drift into a reverie about which song might get the most people I love out on the dance floor to celebrate together. And forget trying to reconcile my pleasure at the thought of providing for Jonathan's needs with the cultural baggage attached to the word "wife."

Basically, it's an intellectual/emotional stalemate. (Is it at all telling that every time I try to type the word "engagement," I wind up with "en*gag*ment," until Microsoft Word reminds me with that polite little squiggly red line that I've made an error?)

Can you see why it's perfect that Jonathan made the first move?

The ring inside the little hexagonal black leather box—which, in the heat of the moment, we almost forget to open—was more evidence that, where I'm concerned, he just knows what needs to be done. It's different: a big opaque pink ruby set in white gold, discovered at a little vintage jewelry store down the street from his apartment. He picked it out by himself, and wanted to get it sized for the "proper" finger. At the urging of the proprietor, he finagled something from my jewelry box, which he plunked on her counter one day. "Honey, that's an earring," was the woman's bemused reply. (Indeed, it was—a braided silver hoop earring, circa 1992.) Flustered, Jonathan bought it and fled.

It's a funky ring, and sizeable, and at first, I wasn't sure what to think of it, or, really, what to do with it. I didn't know if I should get it sized, or if I even wanted to wear it every day. But it's taken up residence on the middle finger of my left hand, where it fits perfectly, and because I love the story behind it, and because I like how it looks there, I think that's where it will stay.

But if I allow myself to peel back that decision, I find a deeper truth. Wearing it on the "improper" finger gives me more control over its meaning. I can wear it with another ring stacked on top of it, an intricately carved sterling silver snake ring from the '20s, which I purchased myself at that same store, and which I've grown to see as a sort of talisman. I like how the snake is "guarding" my ring; I like the juxtaposition of an object he bought for me and an object I bought myself.

An unconventional ring on an unconventional finger doesn't signal to people that I'm "off the market," but as long as Jonathan's OK with it, I'm not concerned about the impression I'm making on others. But the way a glance at my left hand makes *me* feel is pretty damn important. When I have a wedding ring, and a new identity to match, I'll use the "right" finger. But for now, during this transition period, I want to take my time in becoming.

When it comes to spreading the word, however, there's no such thing as gradual. Sure, there was a moment when we were alone with our secret to keep or tell, a beat of bewilderment and possibility. Should we savor it privately? Run to the phone to book a reception venue? Send out a fleet of carrier pigeons, with little tulle bows on their ankles?

But eventually you have to make one call, and then another, and pretty soon the juggernaut begins to roll. News of an engagement is a force only slightly less powerful than that which binds people to babies and puppies: "When? Where? Tell me everything!" We've gotten cards and gifts and phone calls; it's sweet and flattering but overwhelming. There also have been some negative reactions; friends and family whose first response was less than enthusiastic. I think that because the engagement took people by surprise, many reactions came from the gut, shaped in large part by hopes, desires, victories, and flameouts that had little to do with us.

And that's fine with me. Because another thing I've learned is that this is *not* just about us. On our first post-engagement visit to his hometown of Akron, Ohio, welcomed with love by Jonathan's extended family, I saw in their eyes that they weren't just happy for us, they were truly touched by our decision, in a literal way. It almost immediately had a very real impact on their lives. I now believe that the laws of eminent domain apply in families; that the people who created us have at least some

> I finally understand what people mean
> when they say that marriage belongs to
> the community.

claim on the course of our lives. I finally understand what people mean when they say that marriage belongs to the community.

And so one of my first short-timer takes on the meaning of marriage is that "us two" is an exponent. It quickly gets bigger than you thought possible, with larger and larger concentric circles radiating out from it, and arrows and boxes and footnotes, and everything overlaps, until suddenly the process of getting from engagement to wedding to beyond looks like a blueprint for a thermonuclear reactor.

Or, on brighter days, it looks like instructions for building some magnificent, complex vessel; a sailing ship, a spaceship, maybe even a time machine. And though right now Jonathan and I don't even know which way to hold the plans, let alone how to start building, every day provides a learning opportunity.

F Words of Wisdom

If you've just gotten engaged, and you're not sure what you've gotten into, you're not crazy, and you're not alone.

~

It's not a bad idea to wait a while to share the news of your engagement with family and friends. Sure, if you're bubbling over with happiness, you want to share. But in some ways, it's the last truly private moment of your relationship.

~

An unconventional ring can help make the engagement process more private: You're not wearing a giant, sparkly billboard for your status, in any sense of the word.

~

A piece of this process belongs to your families. Just look into their eyes and you'll see that it's true.

June 30

LEARN BEFORE YOU LEAP

Everything a new fiancée never wanted to know about marriage—and had no clue to ask.

SHORT OF A COUTURE GOWN, is anything as tailor-made for a new fiancée as a reporting assignment at a marriage conference? Getting ready for this year's "Smart Marriages," held in Dallas earlier this month, I was keenly aware that my professional and personal lives might never again be so perfectly aligned, and determined to make the most of it. On the early morning flight out from New York, clutching my green tea and new blue pen, I had that geek-in-heaven, first-day-of-school feeling: There never was a newbie so eager to sit at the feet of gurus and absorb their wisdom.

Three days and a coffee-stained, scribble-filled notebook later, instead of feeling remotely "smart," I felt like I had been given a marriage swirly—like someone had stuck my head in the marital toilet bowl, and flushed. Couldn't see anything, couldn't hear anything, couldn't even think of anything but the mind-bending exercises looming ahead in my own personal copy of "Marital Theory and Practice" (first edition).

> I felt like I had been given a marriage
> swirly—like someone had stuck my
> head in the marital toilet bowl, and
> flushed.

But since coming back to reality, where people don't scuttle back and forth between seminars with titles like "Hot Monogamy" and "Become a Divorce Buster!" while wearing buttons that say "I Love My Husband," I've realized how lucky I was to get a glimpse into that rarified world when I did.

Smart Marriages is a marriage-education conference, meaning it's for people who teach other people how to rise to the challenges of being a husband or a wife. That group includes therapists, educators, psychologists, social scientists, community organizers, the clergy, and even representatives from the government and the military (in which, I learned, the divorce rate is alarmingly on the rise).

The conference presenters included researchers of every stripe, from John Gottman, whose lab in Seattle tries to quantify the power dynamics of arguing couples and chart the resulting emotional damage; to Marline Pearson, who talked about marriage among disadvantaged populations; to Linda Waite, who correlated marriage and physical health. It also included such performers and pundits as John Gray and Pat Love, experts with a capital "E."

The one thing all attendees have in common is that they're idealists: They believe men and women can learn how to make marriage better once they're in it, and, more relevant for me, should take the time to explore what they're really getting into before they commit. The theory goes that strong, well-fed marriages are good not only for individuals, but also for society— and no one who's ever spent a minute with an angry, frightened child of a one-parent home would argue with that.

Never one for skipping class, I attended all the keynotes, and, with a staggering eighteen choices for every time slot, agonized over my workshops. I learned Janis Abrams Spring's take on forgiveness for extreme situations—when the other party is unrepentant, or dead. (Her message: Let go and save yourself.) I heard Gary Chapman talk about the "Five Love Languages," and how we don't always know how to recognize and interpret the caring other people are sending our way. I saw Scott Stanley present some startling research on the shaky fate of marriages in which the couple cohabitates first, and I felt great relief when I learned that even though Jonathan and I plan to move in together before we marry, our odds look OK. (The key, according to Stanley, is making a conscious decision to marry beforehand, rather than sliding into it once you've already merged homes.)

But my favorite presenter was Barry McCarthy, a professor of psychology at American University. Listening to McCarthy, also a therapist, author of a book for newlyweds called *Getting It Right the First Time*, and straight shooter who spoke candidly about his own background and marriage ("My wife was forty-five minutes late for the wedding because her parents were trying to talk her out of it."), one thing became very clear to me: Getting married is a choice. Especially today, thanks to progress, and prosperity, and the generations of American women before me who have worked for change, it's an elective. And because it's something I'm deliberately, consciously bringing into being, and because I have so many resources at my disposal, there's no excuse not to invest in it accordingly.

> Everyone is bound to have some strengths *and* some weaknesses, which means no one is perfect, and—joy!— you're no more imperfect than anyone else.

McCarthy has a list of eighteen things that he believes are predictors for the success or failure of a marriage. That's a lot of rules, right? But the great part about his list is that, when he explains it, you don't quake at the thought of everything you're lacking. Instead, you see where you're lucky, where you need to be aware, and where you maybe should make an extra effort. With so many things to think about, everyone is bound to have some strengths *and* some weaknesses, which means no one is perfect, and—joy!—you're no more imperfect than anyone else.

He also believes that if you're doing it right, the first couple years of the marriage should be the toughest—"just like college," he said. That's the time when couples are establishing their style, and their culture; learning how to fight, and how to make up. Getting the kinks out. Making the mold. "It will inoculate you against problems later," McCarthy promised the room, and I lapped it up, breathing a huge sigh of relief about the frequency of fights between Jonathan and me, on a steady upswing since we got engaged.

Looking back at my notes from McCarthy's seminar, I see "sign up for classes with Jonathan" underlined three times. I guess it hadn't occurred to me until that moment that we weren't considering getting premarital counseling of any kind. Sure, there are books we've agreed to leaf through—Susan Piver's *The Hard Questions: 100 Essential Questions to Ask Before You Say "I Do"* has been on the nightstand for weeks—and we've been feeling virtuous about that. And we have good role models in our two sets of still-married folks, so it's not like we're totally oblivious to what a good marriage looks like. But come on: We have no plans for any dedicated study at close range with anyone who has enough experience with marriage to qualify as a teacher or a mentor. Just how, I'm now wondering, do we expect to learn anything at all—or even get a glimmer of what we don't know?

So it's settled. Jonathan and I are going to school. (And yes, I cleared it with him first. Duh—that's gotta be Wife 101, and even I can handle that.) In the words of writer Lauren Winner, whom *Tango*, the relationship magazine I work for, interviewed in our summer 2005 issue, "We take cello lessons. We take yoga. We are open to having instruction in all sorts of endeavors, and yet marriage . . . is something that we've come to think happens behind closed doors." She's right. It's hard to admit that we're going to need some help. But attending to this conference got me one step closer to being OK with that.

So, looking back, I did learn a lot in Dallas. And I mostly enjoyed the chance to be a student again. I did play hooky once, though, I'll admit. I went out into the searing heat, took the DART light rail to Dealey Plaza, and bought a ticket for the Sixth Floor Museum at the Texas School Book Depository.

Jonathan is a bit of a Kennedy assassination savant. He once presented a paper on discrepancies in the medical evidence to seven hundred people at an assassination symposium—when he was sixteen years old. So, naturally, the one thing he wanted me to do on my trip was visit the museum: see the re-created shooter's perch, watch the short films and newsreels, get up close to the artifacts of that sad moment in our history. I enjoyed the visit, but the best part was Jonathan's reaction when I called to tell him where I was. He was thrilled that I had honored his request, and that I now have more insight into his passion.

So as we prepare for our wedding, we'll definitely be signing up for some premarital ed along with the standard ballroom dancing lessons—and I'll be sure to remember the other lesson I learned that weekend: In the school of love, you can get big-time extra credit for field trips.

F Words of Wisdom

You're choosing to get married—you also can choose to take steps to make your marriage last. The sooner you make that a focus, the better, because prevention is always better than cure. It's easy for the wedding to take center stage, but the marriage is what lasts a lifetime.

~

Discuss premarital counseling (a.k.a. marriage education) with your fiancé. With luck, you'll both agree that it's a good idea. If you don't feel like you're ready for class, then pick up a copy of a conversation-starting book, such as *The Hard Questions: 100 Essential Questions to Ask Before You Say "I Do"* by Susan Piver, *1001 Questions to Ask Before You Get Married* by Monica Mendez Leahy, or *Don't You Dare Get Married Until You Read This! The Book of Questions for Couples* by Corey Donaldson. Read them together, and take notes on any problem areas.

~

Read Barry McCarthy's marital-success predictors (below) and see how you score. But don't be afraid—every couple has strengths, and weaknesses. The key is knowing what they are so you can capitalize on the strengths, while addressing and figuring out how to compensate for the things that may trip you up as a couple.

1. You grew up in an intact, functional marriage.
2. Your parents were a good marital and sexual model.
3. Both of your parents function well psychologically, especially your mom if you're a girl, or dad if you're a guy.

4. You're at least twenty-one years old at the time you get married, and not pregnant.

5. You're marrying for positive reasons—to share your life with another person—and not negative ones, such as fear of loneliness, parental pressure, or not being sure how to organize your life.

6. You've known your partner for at least one year on your wedding day.

7. The two of you share similar religious, education, race, and socio-economic backgrounds.

8. You're attracted to each other *and* you have the potential to develop what experts call "mature intimacy."

9. You've thoroughly discussed important life-organization issues: work, money, children, where to live.

10. You have the approval of your families and friends.

11. You see your prospective spouse as a respectful, trusting friend.

12. Neither of you is keeping major secrets from the other.

13. Your bond of respect, trust, and intimacy grows stronger in the first two years of your relationship.

14. You develop a mutually acceptable "couple style."*

---

* *A Word on Couple Styles:* Marriage and family therapy experts have identified four primary "styles" in which couples interact. It doesn't matter one bit which you are—all can be equally successful; all have unique strengths and challenges—as long as you've found one that works for both of you.

"Complementary," a.k.a. "You say po-tay-toh, I say po-tah-toh—and that's totally cool."

"Conflict-Minimizing," a.k.a. "Don't rock the boat."

"Best Friend," a.k.a. "It's twins!"

"Emotionally Expressive," a.k.a. "Drama-rama."

15. You wait at least two years before the birth of your first child, and that child is planned and wanted.

16. You develop a comfortable, sexually functional relationship.

17. You have the ability to deal with differences and conflicts.

18. Both of you maintain positive, realistic marital expectations.

Adapted from "Factors Which Predict Marital Success" by Barry McCarthy, Ph.D., author of *Getting It Right the First Time*. Reprinted with permission.

<u>*July 10*</u>

EX MARKS THE TENDER SPOT

Whose responsibility is it to make sure that your ex finds out (gently) that you're getting married?

THIS IS THE CHAPTER that I almost didn't write. I lived every word and nuance in it a hundred times over, but got gutless about putting it down on paper. Even now, I'm typing with that shifting feeling in my stomach, treading on the wobbly writer's territory where you wonder if you're making your living at the expense of your life.

But I'll publish first and beg forgiveness later because the other morning, I had breakfast with a publicist. I ate eggs, and she ate oatmeal. We talked about the product she was promoting. And then the talk turned to personal matters, and—with the instant intimacy people in public relations seem to have with strangers, that weirdly seductive mix of frankness and pluck—she told me she'd been "medicated for three days."

The reason?

Her ex-boyfriend is getting married.

And she heard the news from someone else.

I made a sympathetic noise, then was quiet for a moment. I've been the third party who knew that a friend's ex was tying

the knot. And, as I sheepishly admitted to the medicated publicist, I didn't tell my friend.

"I would have killed you!" she shrieked.

As she would have had reason to do. I took what can only be described as the easy way out. But, for what it's worth, it wasn't all that easy. If you know that someone's ex is getting married and you also know the ex who hasn't told them, you are in an uncomfortable, convoluted situation, full of conflicting loyalties and reluctance to cause pain.

Maybe I'm writing this as penance for not telling. Or maybe I want to point out that the silent third party isn't the worst offender in that mess. I believe it boils down to this: If the news of your engagement is going to make waves—and you know whether it will, and with whom, so don't try to deny it—you absolutely must report it yourself. It's when people don't do the right thing right away that other people get sloshed by their messy wake.

After the breakfast, I thought about my experience with being kept in the dark, by the exes who hadn't told me they were getting married.

If we go back to my first brushes with this situation, we find a pretty pileup of fantasies and delusions. I didn't do bad breakups; I was a collector, one of those girls who liked to think she had all of 'em within arm's reach. Like charms on a charm bracelet, fixed in time, and dangling just a little. Sure, any one of my exes was probably dating someone else. No, he wouldn't drop everything and come running back to me at a moment's notice. Hell, I wouldn't even want him to. But I was pretty sure that, deep down, *he* wanted to, and that was all that mattered.

As we all moved into marrying age, I even got some perverse satisfaction from the fact that my former flames remained single. Like no cavities, "no married exes" was something to brag about. By the time I learned that my first real high school boyfriend had gotten married, he was already divorced. The same thing happened with another ex from that era. Who needed more proof that I was unforgettable? (And so who cared that they hadn't delivered the news personally?)

I'm not proud of that thinking, but it's mine, even though it dates from a less secure, less in-the-moment era of my life. Since then, I've heard several exes' Big News through the grapevine, with nothing but good feelings. And I'd be thrilled to hear more, by e-mail, phone, or Sunday newspaper. Most of my more mature, sanguine attitude comes from my joy and optimism about my current romantic situation, but it's also partially due to lack of scar tissue: Through the grace of good timing, none of my exes' marriages touched a raw nerve.

When it came to delivering the Big News of my own engagement, though, I found I had a nerve or two. And timing definitely was not on my side.

Four months before my first date with Jonathan, I had moved out of the apartment I had been sharing with Sam, my boyfriend of almost four years. Sam and I grew up in the same hometown, met years later in Chicago, moved one-two to San Francisco, then packed up together for a new life in New York: graduate school for him, a new career for me, one apartment to hold us both. It was the first step in what we imagined would be a long life together. Not much more than a year later, we were saying our good-byes—fondly, sadly, and definitively.

According to my datebook, I told Sam that Jonathan and I were getting married ten days after the proposal. Sam may not have popped into my head on day one, but I was vividly aware of his presence on the nine that followed.

I had thought about him all the time during the first year of my relationship with Jonathan. I called it the "Sam echo." Every time Jonathan and I would hit a milestone, big or small, I'd reflexively wonder, "Was this how it was with Sam?" Every time we'd have a "first"—first vacation, first parental visit, first argument—I'd check myself. "Did I feel this way with Sam? How was it different?" I hated that echo, because it felt nothing but bad: wrong, tainted, mean to Sam, unfair to Jonathan.

But it also felt inevitable, and I let my girlfriends soothe me. "What else are you supposed to be thinking about?" they'd say. "It's natural to compare."

After the proposal, when Jonathan and I headed into new territory, the echo morphed into a different kind of noise. I felt guilty that we were doing this so soon after Sam and I had broken up, and so my conscience clanged like an old radiator. The mere thought of one of the many friends we have in common triggered a shrill warning bell—Sam might hear the news from someone other than me. And there was a constant background drone emanating from some deep place, because I just couldn't rest, much less move forward with wedding planning, until he knew.

I think that was partly because I knew that telling it straight was the "right" thing to do in a take-your-medicine kind of

> Call me sentimental or silly, but I believe in fresh starts, and in the power of good intentions.

way, but also because I want to do everything "right" as I transition into this new life. To bungle telling Sam would be a black mark on something that, my distaste for bridal clichés notwithstanding, I honestly do want to be as snowy white as possible. Call me sentimental or silly, but I believe in fresh starts, and in the power of good intentions.

Of course, the trick with good intentions is executing well. (The road to hell, and all that.) So I thought about how Sam operates: He's dignified, honest, caring, genteel. Then I turned it around. How would I feel if he came to me with that news? How would I want to find out? Since we live in the same city, e-mail seemed cowardly; the phone, only slightly less so. The best way to do it would be in person. But that also would be the most uncomfortable. So I dragged my feet.

Of course, life has a way of shoving you in front of the things you need to attend to, and if you stall, it just shoves harder. Some friends who were moving threw themselves an impromptu going-away bash. I got the e-mail on a Friday morning about the party that night, one week after Jonathan's proposal. Most of the people who might be there, the hosts included, hadn't yet heard the news.

I suspected that Sam would be there—he was on the invitation—but hoped he would not. There was no time to tell him in any remotely suave way in the hours that were rapidly ticking away. And though it couldn't get much worse than telling him at the party, getting through the night without him finding out would be tough.

I got there early. Sam arrived literally on my heels. I had a drink. Our hosts were there, tired from packing; I wanted to tell them, but I held my tongue. I was alternately grateful that the situation seemed to be under control and resentful about this blot on my bridely prerogative—in another universe, I'd already be blissfully buzzed from celebratory toasts.

Jonathan arrived. We exchanged panicked glances. Other friends in the know arrived. They whispered queries. Had we done any planning? I was bursting. I had another drink. Our hosts were leaving the next morning in a moving truck, headed for California. They wouldn't have a chance to slip up, I told myself. Selfishness won. I whispered in their ears. Their eyes bulged, but their mouths stayed closed.

At the end of the evening, Sam still didn't know. Disaster averted, I resolved to tell him as soon as possible. The following Monday, I e-mailed to ask if he wanted to have lunch, and we made a date for the next day.

We got burgers and fries and sat outside in a patch of spring sunshine. I ached—a nonspecific, everywhere sort of ache, like on a cellular level—and my throat felt funny. We made small talk. I choked down some food. I psyched myself up. Bite. Chew. Swallow. Spit it out.

> You don't stop understanding someone
> just because you've broken up. And you
> don't stop expecting to be understood.

"I'm getting married."

He hadn't heard it from anyone else. But his face registered no surprise, as I knew it wouldn't. He was reserved, but polite, gracious, and congratulatory—just as I expected him to be. He didn't tell me how he really felt about the situation. I know he never will.

The familiarity of his responses almost hurt worse than telling him. You don't stop understanding someone just because you've broken up.

And you don't stop expecting to be understood. Therein lies the root of the publicist's anguish, I suppose, and that of anyone who doesn't hear it from the source. We can't always control who we fall in and out of love with. But we can try to treat everyone with love.

F WORDS OF WISDOM

Take a deep breath, and think about your former flames. Now make a list of anyone who would be less than genuinely happy to hear the news that you're getting married.

Remove the names of anyone on whom you have taken out a restraining order. Then start dialing.

~

E-mail and—God forbid—text messaging are not appropriate ways to deliver the news. In person, or over the phone, is best. Instant messaging might be OK, depending on the circumstances. The key is to be "there" when you break the news, to make yourself available to hear his response, and respond in kind. Without that back-and-forth, no one can get closure.

~

If you are among the surprisingly large group of fiancées who decided to take the plunge shortly after emerging from another long-term relationship, it may be extra hard to break the news, but it's also especially important.

~

The bottom line: Treat your exes as you'd want them to treat you if the situation were reversed.

July 27

READY FOR YOUR CLOSE-UP?

For a while, it's all kisses, champagne, and let's-see-the-ring squeals. Then reality hits: You actually have to plan a wedding.

I KNOW SOME COUPLES leap swiftly and gracefully from "will you?" to "where do we sign?" on the contract for a reception venue, but that hasn't been us. We've deliberately taken some time off between the engagement and starting to plan our wedding. And now that we are beginning to think about planning—well, let's just say that we aren't looking to set any land-speed records. Why? Because it's hard to know where to begin. Because for certain major questions—such as where to have it—there's no obvious answer. And because I've been dragging my feet.

It's a personality thing. I think, and then I plan, and then I act. Or, more accurately, I think, and then I think, and then I think (OK, you can call it worrying), and then someone makes a crack about what a head case I am and so I finally do something.

In this situation, there are a few things that are especially fun to chew on.

First—and don't stone me for this—I'm ambivalent about weddings. Actually, it's more like schizophrenia: I can be the biggest sap alive, and if I love the bride and groom and the ceremony pulls the right strings, I'm reduced to a weeping, snotty mess. On the other hand, I have a healthy whatever-wave-I-am feminist streak, and I'm also very skeptical of the "Wedding-Industrial Complex," the materialism it perpetuates, and a lot of the "traditions" brides and grooms feel compelled to follow. Some weddings leave me rolling my eyes.

Second, I have a love-hate relationship with being the center of attention. (And being engaged can feel like one long moment in the hot seat.)

Third, you can't start planning until you more or less know what you want. And it's taking some time, on both a conscious and a subconscious level, to rifle through the old mental database of wedding-related expectations, hopes, and ideas, and decide what I'd like to include in our plans, and what's past its expiration date. I remember drifting off to sleep imagining my wedding day when I was as young as eight or nine years old. That's a lot of history.

Plus, there's a schism in it, dating back to the summer I was sixteen, and working as a fill-in receptionist at my dad's office. I had a co-worker there, a sweet girl maybe three years older than me, who was about to get married. She indulged my starry-eyed questions about dresses, flowers, and cake, but she also made it very clear that, to her, those things were secondary: The prize her eyes were on was marriage. It was my first glimpse under the veil of the wedding-day fantasies that had been running rampant since the minute I learned how to make Barbie and Ken hold hands (among other things), and it made me feel, well, childish. Suddenly I saw shadows of things like resolve and hard work and lifetime commitment—which I had formerly associated with Grown-Ups, a.k.a. people who were decidedly not me—behind the menu choices and color schemes, and it chastened me. I was awestruck that someone who was close to me in age could be light years more worldly. Since then, a part of me has been terrified that wanting a wedding, or, at least, wanting it *too much*, is silly and shallow.

More than a decade later, I finally have some insight into what might have been going through my co-worker's head. I don't doubt her sincerity, but I may have given too much weight to her message. Perhaps she adopted the mantra that her marriage was what was really important—and saw fit to repeat it to me at every opportunity—because she was struggling to keep her priorities in order.

The wedding industry, with its magazines, books, Web sites, TV shows, bridal expos, and vendors of every stripe, is even more powerful, seductive, and sly than I suspected—and now I'm their target. Think about it: you're a boggled bride, struggling to reconcile half-buried childhood fantasies about your Big Day with your grown-up life and its realities. If life were a sci-fi flick, the wedding industry would be played by a hologram of a brisk, efficient woman in a Chanel suit, promising you the perfect event, complete with romance, class, and a side of (no strings attached!) warm maternal guidance. *We've got this under control, darling. Right this way . . .*

> If life were a sci-fi flick, the wedding
> industry would be played by a hologram
> of a brisk, efficient woman in a Chanel
> suit, promising you the perfect event,
> complete with romance, class, and a side
> of (no strings attached!) warm maternal
> guidance.

It's your fairy godmother. It's your Obi-Wan Kenobi. It's no contest! The minute you make that first, tentative foray onto theknot.com (where, by the way, you can't register without a wedding date), it's bibbity-bobbity-boo!—and you're swept away by a soothing river of peonies and silk shantung.

Here's another theory: An engagement requires so much heavy emotional lifting—letting go of your single self, learning to take someone else into consideration in most everything you do, redefining what you consider your "family," thinking seriously about your long-term future—that you focus on something that is comparatively manageable: the wedding. You can't exactly corral your future happiness, health, home, goals, careers, lifestyle, family issues, and possible progeny onto a checklist divided into three-month intervals. Maybe that's why so many of us brides make our peace with Big Bridesmaid and drink the champagne-flavored Kool-Aid.

Which brings me to a final, more recent fantasy: that Jonathan and I are going to be able to do this Our Way, and that our wedding will be Totally Unique. I think it's a particular affliction of my generation of American women (and men, too, to some extent). We're always looking for the newest, best thing, and because "copycat" is just as horrifying a slur as it was when we were seven, we want to put a personal stamp on the nuptials, make them quirky, mix-and-match, one-of-a-kind.

Don't get me wrong: having the freedom and the means to make a wedding uniquely yours is a wonderful thing. But the cynic in me can't help but frame it as a "Mad Libs" scenario: Scene opens [pick one: at the beach/on a mountaintop/in the desert] where your [insert pet species here] is wearing a [tutu *or* fedora *or* lei], trotting down an aisle strewn with [your state flower] to the strains of [instrument indigenous to the country where you studied abroad in college].

And so on, and so forth.

Viewed that way, the "custom" wedding quickly becomes . . . pretty standard. Not to mention that pulling it together can be one hundred times more stressful than falling back on tradition.

Clearly, I could filibuster for ages. But after a while, you start to feel a little sheepish if you can't come up with a date when people ask, and you *do* really want to make the thing official, and you *don't* have cold feet (quite the opposite, really). And even if some quick, super-intimate affair (what Jonathan and I have referred to as "the nuclear option") would be simpler (oh, how much simpler!) and *could* be sweeter in some ways, thinking of foregoing the pleasures of a traditional wedding makes me sad.

So when I drop down into the muck of ambivalence, I pull myself out with this thought: I don't want to look back on this moment, this incredible rite of passage, with anything resembling a regret. And though it's taken a few months of deliberation, inquiry, and soul-searching, I'm becoming more confident that we can figure out how to craft a relaxed, fun, unique, affordable, meaningful, memorable event centered on the act of exchanging vows in front of all the people we love. Much of that is down to Jonathan, who is helping me feel less self-conscious about participating in what, on a bad day, I could easily write off as a giant cliché. He's got a simple, heartfelt, decidedly non-neurotic approach that takes me back to being the sniffly girl in a pew, watching something beautiful unfold . . . which, as I realize when I can get out of my own way, is exactly where I want to be.

Well, almost exactly. I'll be a performer this time, instead of in the audience, and I'm coming to terms with that. The next step is finding the perfect stage.

F Words of Wisdom

It's a great idea to take some time—several months, even, if you like—to just soak up the idea of being engaged before you begin to tackle wedding planning. It's helpful to set a "kickoff" date, then try (it's hard, but try) to relax and not obsess too much about it until that date arrives.

~

The second you get engaged, all things bridal and beautiful may beckon like sirens at the edge of a bucolic pool. But don't feel like you have to jump in before you're ready! Try to block out the wedding-industry roar and listen for the quieter voice inside your own head, the one that will lead you where you want to go. There's almost as much peer pressure in the world of the bride as there was in junior high! Luckily you now have more practice at trusting your gut and diverging from the crowd.

~

If you're feeling overwhelmed by the idea of the planning process, remember that it's just like any other project: Getting started is the hardest part.

~

Planning stress can rub off on your relationship. That's normal, and manageable. Try to keep things in perspective: You wouldn't be going through this rose petal–strewn hell if you didn't love each other and want to spend your lives together!

~

People will ask you a trillion nosy but (usually) well-intentioned questions. If these questions make you uncomfortable, confer with your fiancé and come up with a polite stock response that both of you can use to sweetly, but firmly, change the subject, e.g., "Oh, we're just relishing being engaged for the moment—we aren't even going to start thinking about planning until after the new year," or, "Thanks for your input, but you know, we've made all the key decisions and want to keep them a surprise for our guests until the time comes." You get the idea. It's important that the two of you are armed with the same message—at all stages of the planning process—especially where your families are concerned. It's a great opportunity to learn how to present a united front.

August 6

PLAN W

When, where, who, and how (much)? Getting married can feel like solving a puzzle—and it's not just about the wedding.

A FTER A LONG-PLANNED TRIP to Paris with two dear col-lege friends, I finally felt ready to get down to it: planning the wedding. Jonathan and I are so blessed—with health, great families, ample resources, lots of friends—that there really aren't any significant limits. Neither of us has an overwhelming vision of exactly how we want it to be. We could make this cel-ebration just about anything we want, anywhere we want. That kind of freedom is exhilarating—for about thirty seconds. Then it's paralyzing.

So we decided that what we needed was a peg to hang things on, a macro decision from which all the micro decisions would naturally flow. We quickly realized that there were four main interlocking elements: the date, the place (with the venue as a subset of that), the number of guests, and the budget. Date and place are interdependent for reasons of weather and availability. Size of guest list can dictate place, and vice versa; to some extent, date can impact how many people will show. Budget rules all.

> We could make this celebration just about anything we want, anywhere we want. That kind of freedom is exhilarating—for about thirty seconds. Then it's paralyzing.

Like solving a Sudoku puzzle, we began filling in the obvious. Most any date would do. Our only criterion—and this is arbitrary—was to marry before either of us turned thirty, so before June 17, 2006, Jonathan's birthday. Easy enough. Place was less arbitrary, and much more complicated. We didn't have history, geography, or religion to help us narrow the field: no childhood house of worship in common, nor country club, not even a shared alma mater. I grew up in Nebraska, went to college in Chicago, and also spent a few years in San Francisco. He grew up in Ohio, and went to college in Indiana. We both have friends and family all over the country; we both have elderly grandparents who don't travel well. The one constant in our lives is New York, but few things in life are more expensive or complicated than a New York wedding, so we ruled that out almost immediately.

At first, we thought that an exotic destination wedding would be the way to go: If the location was inconvenient for everyone, then we'd never be accused of playing favorites. I got a wild hair about Puerto Rico; specifically the island of Vieques, a lush green splotch off the coast of the big island. It sounded untouched and exotic and a little rough around the edges, a place of natural beauty and quirky culture where everyone could have a really good, affordable time.

We flew to San Juan, then took the long car ride to Fajardo and the short, choppy flight to Vieques. We loved everything about it: the battered jeep we rented to traverse the winding roads, the wild horses grazing in the ditch, the nighttime boat ride and swim in a bioluminescent bay full of single-cell organisms that dripped like tiny glowing stars from our fingertips, the impossibly pure, impossibly empty white-sand beaches. Everything. But what made a rustic, romantic weekend getaway for two would be a logistical nightmare for a wedding. We had a hard time figuring out where on the island we could bring the event in under budget, and a hard time justifying asking our guests to take tiny planes or an inconvenient ferry—with attached costs that, in aggregate, were not all that cheap after all.

Ultimately, we didn't like the thought that people we love might be priced or inconvenienced out of being able to see us wed. Even for the "would attend at any cost" crowd, it started to seem selfish to commandeer so much of their vacation time and budgets.

Bye-bye, Vieques.

Which, irrationally, pissed me off. And made me feel depressed. I guess I had sunk a lot of hope into that one idea, so when it was gone, I was bereft. We were back to square one, and time was ticking away. We scrambled for an alternative, flirting with a beach wedding in Cape May, New Jersey. And though we had initially rejected Nebraska, my home state, outright, we revisited that idea, too. Frustrated and impatient to make progress, Jonathan and I found ourselves bickering a lot. Not to mention that we have two sets of parents who, for different reasons and in different ways, wanted and needed to know what was going on.

Which brings me to the issue of money, for me the most heart wrenching. I'm almost thirty years old. I've been financially independent (if you don't count a few minor lapses and major gifts) since I graduated from college. I really think I should be paying for my own wedding. But the fact is, I can't afford the kind of wedding we want, and neither can Jonathan. And we're just selfish enough (or America 2005 enough) to put our wants above our means. So we're looking to our parents. And because of my sentimental, old-fashioned streak, and probably some kind of pride as well, that means my parents.

They've been wonderful, and offered us a generous amount. It's hard stuff to talk about; we've all survived by saying as little as possible. However, because we're taking their money, I feel we need to take their direction, too. Or, rather, respect their wishes. Some of them, anyway. Or, just be open to what they have to say. Well, OK, at least tell them how we're spending their dough. But really, it's our call. Because they're not getting married, we are. Right?

Around the time we were in the deepest, darkest part of the date/place/budget/size forest, and trying to figure out what we owed to whom, I went to the Smart Marriages conference, as previously mentioned. What I haven't yet told you about is the part that made my mouth drop open in recognition and relief:

> Weddings are about power and money
> and control and loyalty and, of course,
> "family of origin." And all these tensions
> are wrapped up together in the form of
> your first big public test, your first big
> performance, where you are the star,
> dressed up and looking perfect.

the banquet presided over by Bill Doherty, a professor of family science at the University of Minnesota. It was called "Let's Talk About Weddings," and in it Doherty, a longtime marital educator, took his colleagues to task.

Why, he asked them, do marriage-preparation experts insist on ignoring the wedding in their work, when it is a magnet for most of the major issues a couple will face later on? I almost fell off my chair, because the approach he was criticizing was exactly the one I'd been taking: A wedding is just a party; the marriage is what's important. If I can't handle this, I'm a big baby. But no, Doherty said—and confessed that it had struck him like a ton of bricks while helping his daughter and son-in-law plan their recent nuptials—weddings are about power and money and control and loyalty and, of course, "family of origin" (psych-speak for "the in-laws"). And all these tensions are wrapped up together in the form of your first big public test, your first big performance, where you are the star, dressed up and looking perfect. (*And, by the way, why are you crying, Bridezilla?*)

Turns out that all the stuff you've tried to tune out—the family issues, the money worries, the hundred different challenges a wedding can present, along with their sidecars full of anger, sadness, or fear—by fervently believing it's really "your day" and "all about you" show up at the party, after all.

If acknowledging how heavily loaded the wedding itself can be is new to people working in the relationship field, I can stop beating myself up for feeling conflicted. I can't tell you how much better Doherty's speech made me feel.

Getting over the Vieques disappointment—letting go of a fantasy, and making space for something more real—has helped, too. So has trying very hard to be patient with ourselves, and with our families, as we take these gradual, clumsy first steps.

Of course, finally deciding, after all that fuss, that the perfect place for our wedding *is* my home state after all—and wondering why I didn't see it sooner—has brought me a good deal of peace, as well as a delicious feeling of anticipation.

As has a souvenir from that trip to Paris: five meters of lace, impulsively purchased in a shop off the rue du Faubourg St.-Honoré. Since we still don't know a lot about how our wedding will look, it could just as easily wind up a tablecloth as a wedding dress. But right now it's a powerful totem tucked in tissue, pure white and full of promise.

So while we still don't have a guest list, or musicians, or a menu, or even an inkling of how the ceremony will come together, we do have a few things going for us:

We have the lace.

We have one wedding magazine, a gift from my friend Joanne. (The *Martha Stewart Weddings* Tenth Anniversary Issue, no less.)

We have a place: A beautiful, humble little Nebraska barn.

And we have a date: May 20, 2006.

Puzzle solved. Now where's that Sunday *New York Times* crossword?

F WORDS OF WISDOM

Unless the answer is immediately obvious to both of you, choosing the wedding venue probably will be the most angst-ridden part of the planning process. Don't get despondent if you find yourself upset, and/or fighting with your fiancé.

~

Try to be flexible—don't invest too much in any one idea. It's smart to have a list of several acceptable options, akin to "safeties" when you were applying to college. You want to avoid being devastated if your first choice falls through.

~

Another good way to stave off dangerously high expectations, analysis paralysis, delusions of grandeur, and other subspecies of bride brain is to strictly limit your consumption of wedding magazines. That may seem harsh, as everyone deserves a proper binge from time to time, especially on something that has such a short season in one's life. But they really are all the same, and so you only need so many copies. The local magazines often are more useful than the national ones, because they have information you can use along with page after page of pretty pictures. Similarly, though The Knot.com is a good source for local ideas and vendors, try not to get too sucked in to its community features, or the descriptions of other couples' nuptials. And if you've really got it bad, try cutting out the celebrity newsweeklies. Tabloids are chock full of hidden wedding nonsense of the worst kind: celebrity-wedding nonsense.

~

(S)He who holds the purse strings will (should?) get involved. Prepare yourself for some awkward conversations about money, something that's awfully difficult to discuss frankly under any circumstances, and even more so when it comes to weddings. And let's just get it out there: Everything wedding-related is more expensive than you can possibly imagine. Saving money requires some serious resourcefulness. Prioritize, and skimp on the things that are less important.

~

Almost everybody loves the *idea* of a destination wedding. But really think it through. How much will you be asking of your guests? Know that this choice inevitably will wreak havoc with your numbers on either the front end, or the back. If you want to invite a lot of people, it's much harder to predict and plan for how many actually will come. If the destination element means you have to limit the guest list at the outset, prepare for the inevitable hurt feelings. And try as hard as you can to visit the proposed site before making a decision. If nothing else, it's a great excuse for a weekend getaway.

~

Ditto the idea of a wedding over a holiday weekend—you may think you're sparing your guests a vacation day, but those long weekends often already are loaded up with long-standing plans or family obligations. At the very least, poll your nearest and dearest before you book such a weekend.

~

People say it all the time, and maybe you've even said it to yourself: "It's just a party." But it's not. Even the most prosaic decisions can be loaded with emotions you don't expect. Bill Doherty and his daughter have teamed up to offer educational materials aimed at helping engaged couples and their parents manage the considerable stress of wedding planning. Learn more at www.thefirstdance.com.

~

On all fronts, try to be flexible, and know that wonderful weddings come together in all kinds of ways.

September 1

SOMETHING IN THE WAY SHE MOVES

Studies warn about moving in together before you get married. But the lessons to be learned from cohabitation aren't that black and white.

IT'S THE ONE-MONTH ANNIVERSARY of "Jonathan's apartment" becoming "our place," and I wonder—could *this* be the biggest event of the whole process? Good-bye, days of whole-bottle-of-wine-to-yourself and roommates; hello the rest of your life. It's definitely taking a good deal of energy to make the adjustment, for me at least. There's just so much more to think about now, all these living-together and home-keeping issues, as well as financial issues related to living expenses, which seem to pop out around every corner.

I suppose it feels extra significant because we're taking all of it in a lump: the home-related irritants, power struggles, and ideological differences mixed with the identity shifts and wedding-planning bugaboos that engagement brings. But with every new question that arises, I'm happier and happier that we decided to move in together between our engagement and our marriage. I want to figure this stuff out now, and show up on our wedding

day with a working knowledge of what our future home life will be like—not a headful of unanswered questions.

As I've mentioned before, there's research that shows cohabiting before marriage doesn't bode well for the strength of a union, or even for the odds of winding up married at all—much to the dismay, goes the theory, of women who think cohabiting is a giant step toward the altar. (Men, it seems, don't usually see it in quite those terms.) But that research also says that if you move in *after* you're engaged, you're exempt from these grim predictions; your odds rise to compare with those of people who didn't cohabit before tying the knot.

I'm inclined to see these findings as part right-wing propaganda and part common sense. It's logical that two people who move in together in lieu of making the more binding marital commitment may not have matching expectations about where that relationship is going. It's equally possible that two people who have every intention of getting married may start living together, determine that they loathe each other, and break up.

Perhaps a cannier stress test for potential lifelong commitment is not necessarily the *moving in* with someone, but the *moving* itself. And I mean *moving* moving, not hiring someone else to move for you. Think about it: Is there anything more awful, more stressful—more primitive, even? All that grunting and lifting and getting extremely sweaty and dirty. All the orchestrating and scheduling and erratic driving of ancient U-Hauls.

And is there anything that reveals more about a person's values, about his or her style? Do they procrastinate on the pack-

> Perhaps a cannier stress test for potential
> lifelong commitment is not necessarily
> the *moving in* with someone, but the
> *moving* itself.

ing? How do they handle it when items are inevitably misplaced or broken? What dark secrets get turned up when the closets are emptied and the couch cushions removed? If they lean on the labor of friends, how lavishly do they reward those friends for their toil? If they do use movers, how do they treat them? (You learn so much about a person watching him or her interact with anyone who earns an hourly wage.)

I firmly believe that you can see how organized, careful, strong, tidy, disciplined, and generally good-natured a person is when you watch them move. Me? I don't score so well. And since I was the one doing the moving—cramming my stuff into Jonathan's nice but small apartment—I'll take more than half the blame for the debacle that marked the start of our cohabitation.

One thing it revealed was a major style difference. Evidently, I do the long, Chicken Little windup to a big event. He's better at staying cool in the approach, but freaks out closer to the fact. (I actually have a new nickname for him—D.R., for Delayed Reaction. But then again, delayed from what? My hair-trigger early-response system?)

The move was a good dry run for the wedding, I think. I got

stressed and cranky beforehand, anticipating how tiring it would be, how tricky to make everything fit, how grubby, how hot.

In contrast, he was unfazed, almost merry. "What's the big deal? It'll be fine."

Then we got started, and during the actual move, he was grump city. "The dresser is too heavy." "There's no way we'll fit all this stuff in here!" "This sucks."

I tried not to say "I told you so," but, as I mentioned before, I'm a lousy sport about moving.

So I cajoled, and he groaned, and we both sighed, and stomped around. We also learned a good bit about each other's persistence, and our tolerance for discomfort and pain. If moving reveals how much someone can take, I can maybe take too much.

I can definitely be a bit of a masochist. And because I'm hard on myself, I'm often too hard on the people around me. Thanks to my family, this includes some very, very high expectations around the home. My dad is the ultimate household-task stoic. He does it before you knew you wanted it done, and (almost always) without complaining. The joke in our family is that the minute you walk through the door, Larry's asking you to strip so he can put your clothes in the laundry. Call it hyperactivity or obsessive-compulsive disorder, but in the realm of domestic harmony those are helpful conditions.

Jonathan comes from wholly different stock. At his family gatherings, I hear old jokes about Jewish carpenters, and tales of fixing things with duct tape and golf tees.

Moving was just the beginning of a long,
perhaps endless, negotiation.

I suppose the move was just the beginning of a long, perhaps endless, negotiation. I know I've done most of the hammering over the past month. To be fair, we've both done some cooking and cleaning. We're nowhere near divvying up our domestic duties to my satisfaction, though, and I anticipate that it will take a while before we get into a rhythm.

We're still nowhere near settled in, either, and we've definitely done some arguing about what goes where, what to keep, what gets tossed. One thing I'm just realizing is that we're coming at this from completely different perspectives. He's being occupied, and I'm the conqueror encroaching on his space. I have a hard time knowing how much room I can take up, because the space was already pretty full when I got here, especially since he hasn't had to go through the pruning and sorting process that automatically happens when you move. I'm finding it difficult to get him to throw things out retroactively. I'm also resenting that I'm having to ask him to do it at all, but I can understand how it doesn't feel essential to spend a Saturday afternoon filing if you're not about to have to pack up and move.

As far as decorating goes, you could say we're squabbling about that, too—if you consider a wastebasket a decorative accent. Once I got my major stuff put away and started taking stock of the space, I realized that he had outfitted this six-hundred-square-foot studio apartment with five different waste-baskets. I don't even want to think about the feng shui ramifications—all I know is that I couldn't go anywhere without tripping over a barrel of trash, and it was annoying. He liked the convenience, and the basketball practice: You could basically throw something away from any spot in the apartment. But I was able to negotiate him down to three. With any luck, we'll end up keeping two.

Eventually, we'll enter into discussions of less utilitarian things, like throw pillows, and his leaning-tower-of-Ikea lamps. In the meantime, I'm taking notes, learning things you can't know about someone until you live together. For instance: He doesn't simply enjoy watching infomercials, he often needs to be talked out of ordering the products. But perhaps I should just let him send away for whatever he wants. It wouldn't be long before we needed a bigger apartment. Which, of course, would mean another move—and another opportunity to explore the strange nooks and crannies of each other's mind.

F WORDS OF WISDOM

Yes, waiting until after you're married to move in together is old fashioned. Still, some experts—and, honestly, common sense—suggest that it's healthiest for your relationship if you have an officially sanctioned bond in place before combining households. If you're a firm believer in trial runs, moving in after the engagement but before the wedding is a good way to hedge your bets.

~

Moving into a new place that didn't previously belong to either of you is probably the cleanest, fairest start to your life in a shared space.

~

It may sound like torture, but if you can do the move without hiring a moving company, you really will get the most out of the exercise (pun intended). Think of it as another kind of premarital education!

~

Some couples have epic decorating battles; some combine possessions smoothly and with no squabbles. If you're among the former, try the "whoever cares most, wins" method of settling an argument over that trophy fish, La-Z-Boy, or polka-dotted shower curtain. One person almost always feels more strongly than the other, and it's hard to know what kind of emotions someone has tied up in a particular object. If there's something you truly can't stand to look at, suggest registering for a replacement—then choose it together.

September 27

GOOD-BYE, SUPERWOMAN

*Just because you can do anything he can do (better),
doesn't mean you should.*

My coffee-cart guy doesn't miss much—the way he says "good morning" is a remarkably accurate barometer of how successfully I've put myself together that day—so of course he noticed my overnight bag this morning.

"Are you coming or going?"

"Going"

"Where?"

"Chicago."

"I'm going to Chicago today, too! What time are you leaving?"

"Ummmm. Around four? I think?"

I had no idea what time my plane was leaving—or even what airline I was flying—and realizing that gave me a jolt. Jonathan booked the tickets, got the e-mail confirmation, printed our boarding passes, and told me what time to meet him on the subway to get to the airport.

I had zero control over the situation, and I felt fine.

If you're wired anything like I am, you'll know what I'm

talking about when I say that's remarkable. I come from the school of "if you want the job done right, do it yourself... because there are innumerable ways some other asshole could fuck it up." Of course, everyone else who breathes air falls into the "some other asshole" category, except my father, from whom I inherited this charming trait. Of course, I've honed it in my own way over the years. But it must be genetic, because I see it in my brother, Brad, too. We're not just skeptics—we're borderline control freaks, pretty darn sure that we're smarter and more capable than everyone else.

But, astonishingly, I'm realizing that in Jonathan I trust.

There have been moments that make my default DIY setting look rational. For instance, the time he booked the return flight of a New Year's ski trip, our first real vacation together, for the wrong day, necessitating an overnight in Denver with his aunt Susan.

That trip sparked a surprising confession: Jonathan's dubious track record with travel arrangements. Out came a litany of past mistakes. A history of booking things for the wrong day, of booking trips in reverse (so he's scheduled to fly out of his destination and arrive in his departure city), of only noticing that his passport is expired on the way to the airport, then turning around and going home, only to look again and realize that he had read the date wrong—it's valid after all!—turning around once again, and, of course, missing his flight. We could probably pay the entire wedding bar tab with what he's spent on airline change fees.

When I heard these stories, I had to laugh. I was incredulous.

I had been blithely putting my travel plans in *this guy's* hands? But I never would have known. He'd done a great job for us to that point, and those silly mistakes seemed so out of keeping with his meticulous personality.

So while at other times and places in my life I might have gathered up the reins, thank you very much, and taken over from there, I continue to let Jonathan take the lead on most of our travel. I've ceded other things to him, as well, including a good chunk of social scheduling, choosing the music that we listen to at home, the buying of the toilet paper and garbage bags and other things that make the household run.

It only makes sense, as our lives become more and more entwined—financially, socially, and schedule-wise—as well as busier to the point where one person just can't manage it all, especially when you've got wedding planning in the mix. But it's still pretty amazing, because it's a big chunk of responsibility for me to give away, me who's done everything all by myself for more than a decade. And to give it to someone who's demonstrated that, yep, he's fallible ... I must feel really safe. And that's a sign that I'm in the right place.

Still, there are some areas where I just can't let go, and I see battles on the horizon in those areas for years to come, guaranteed. Most of them are domestic. Since we moved in together, there are hundreds more stages on which to play out the question of who's in charge. Some are vast canvases, such as all things financial. As we start to merge money, and plan our future, I can already tell that it will be a challenge to find a decision-making rhythm for things like spending, saving, investing, and real estate—especially because money behaviors are so hard-wired, and, like sex, so rooted in psychology, in how we see ourselves and our place in the world.

For example, I know that we need to set up a budget, and then trust each other to stick to it. But information is power, and even though it's still my own money I'm spending, he's already asking—and I'm already pussyfooting around—how much things cost. (Though what are you supposed to say to a guy who thinks a forty-dollar pair of jeans is outrageous?)

Likewise, we'll need to learn to rely on each other to complete certain financial tasks. I'm happy to let him keep the utilities in his name for now, and I certainly won't hold him to my pay-it-the-minute-you-get-it rule, but I can't imagine a day when finding an overdue electric bill between the couch cushions wouldn't make me apoplectic.

And then there are the smaller arenas where we jockey for position: My fervent conviction that plastic take-out cutlery is not to be chosen over a drawerful of real forks; his declaration that T-shirts must be folded *not in half, not in thirds, but in quarters.* These are small, but not insignificant, parts of who we are. And now those parts are being smashed against each other repeatedly, in an attempt to transmogrify into some new whole. It's *our* forks now, *our* laundry. It's funny how changing little everyday behaviors can feel like such a big deal. I knew it was coming—these are the things all married couples fight about, right?—but I had no idea how it would really feel.

There's also a paradox I'm experiencing, one which I predict will resonate with many women. I feel as if I'm ultimately responsible for the upkeep of our household (if you can call six hundred square feet a household), and that annoys me. Sure, I can delegate, but that still requires management; I still have to determine what needs to be done and put him on it. So it's not like I can completely let go. Beyond that, chances are that the task that I've delegated won't be completed to my satisfaction (I once caught Jonathan scrubbing the bathtub with steel wool) and so I get exasperated thinking about the time and energy I'll have to spend educating him before his work is up to snuff.

But really, he's willing, and smart, and would it actually take that long to show him how I want it done? So, again, this must really be more about control. I should just ask him to do it, and trust that it will happen, even if his methods deviate from my manual.

What's going on here? I've thought about it a lot, and here's where I've landed: In general, I have a hard time accepting help. And not just because of what I said earlier about other people being stupid, but also because my self-image is very much tied up in my strength. The weaker I feel, the less I like myself.

And the heart of the matter is this: If there ever were a time when weakness—dependency—could creep in, it's the time when you're becoming a wife. When you're establishing the patterns of your lives together, if you turn over big decisions, give up financial control, step back when he steps forward, let him do the heavy lifting—you're setting a precedent. At least it seems so to me, at this moment in time.

> If there ever were a time when weakness—dependency—could creep in, it's the time when you're becoming a wife.

So as I'm rushing down a flight of stairs, panting, leaping onto that airport train just in the nick of time, no thanks—I won't let Jonathan take my bag. I don't think I'll *ever* be the kind of woman who wants her husband to carry her bags. So the question, then, is what *can* I let him do? I'm learning that my stiff upper lip can upset him, not because he yearns to be a Sherpa, but because taking care of tasks in our joint life, and taking care of me, helps him feel connected, useful, and secure. I get it, I really do: We're in this together now. Doing things for each other, and letting the other person make some decisions for the both of us, is vital. Weakness and dependency? Optional—a matter of perception, and degree.

These are lessons I have to learn, and I'll keep trying to learn them for a long time to come. In the meantime, I'll take a deep breath, reflect on our successes, and enjoy this relaxing weekend getaway.

What time does our flight leave, again?

F Words of Wisdom

Control is one of the central issues of life, so it's not surprising that control issues are played out again and again in a relationship, in big and small ways. Each half of a couple comes at things from a unique perspective, and approaches tasks differently: It's almost guaranteed that our partners are going to do things their own way, regardless of how much specific direction we give them, and regardless of how ridiculous we think their way is.

~

That is, if they do them at all: There's also the issue of work-load. You hear it again and again: No matter how enlightened the household, the bulk of the work falls on the woman. People offer up myriad theories on why this is so, from the fact that men seem genetically hard-wired not to notice dust bunnies to the idea that first-wave feminism gave women a wrongheaded notion of what it means to be equal, and consequently we run ourselves ragged trying to do everything at the same time. Delegation is an art, and not very many people automatically do it well. But you can get better with practice. And, if necessary, arm and leg restraints.

~

Clearly dividing up responsibilities is your best bet for domestic harmony. Divvy them up however you like, but make sure that neither of you feels overburdened. As to how those tasks get executed, if the procedure chosen by the "doer" is just too annoying for the other person to stomach, and you can't reach a compromise on your own, consider picking up a book to settle the score. I suggest *Henderson's House Rules: The Official Guide to Replacing the Toilet Paper, and Other Domestic Topics of Great Dispute.*

October 11

WAITING TO EXPECT

The pressure begins long before you're legal.

"OOOH, your kids are going to have the narrowest feet."

"I wonder whose complexion they'll get."

"Will they go by Bare, or Cohen?"

It's official. We want kids—not tomorrow, not next year, but someday relatively soon. So once we're finished with this getting-married business, and have taken a reasonable chunk of time for "just us," we're going to try to have them. It's something we've both wanted for a long time. But now that we have an actual plan in place to make our relationship, and any progeny, legit, it all feels more real. Especially when it's all other people can talk about, whether we've shared our intentions with them, or not. (In most cases, we haven't—it's amazing how many people make the assumption.)

Since we got engaged—but only since then—Jonathan and I talk about it, too; about how soon, and how many. At first, we were nervous and shy, as if it wasn't something that should be said out loud. As time has passed, we've relaxed into the topic. Occasionally we even wade out past baby-centric issues, into such forward-looking concepts as the best way to get a kid to

practice the piano, what's a reasonable policy for chores, even our philosophies on curfews—which, of course, don't match. "Can we have a robot that disciplines children so we don't have to?" Jonathan wondered aloud the other day. "You . . . are . . . grounded . . . for . . . twelve . . . days. For an alternative, press two."

Even though we've got that two-years-childfree recommendation from the marriage experts, not to mention our swinging city life, to consider, I've started laying the groundwork. I've gone off the pill; started trying to pinpoint when I'm ovulating. Started pondering all the other things in my life that will need to change before I'll be fit to host another organism for nine months. Thinking about how many I want. Examining my motives for having any at all.

It's an interesting moment in time, culturally, to be almost thirty years old and contemplating trying to get pregnant for the first time. My life and career have been such that it would have been pretty much impossible to have a kid before now. Or, to put it another way, not having a kid before now has allowed me to do a lot of other fantastic things. But it's also crazy to think about how many fertile years have already passed—more than half my life.

Looking at it biologically, it's tempting to, in the words of my friend Mary's gynecologist, "get the party started."

And clearly I'm not the only woman thinking that way. Gina, who's making my wedding dress, and is quite pregnant herself at the moment, told me the other day that "You wouldn't believe how many times I get a call saying, 'Um, I'm going to need some alterations to my dress.'" She mentioned one woman in particular, deathly afraid of being unable to conceive, who started in vitro fertilization during her engagement and was substantially pregnant with twins on her wedding day.

It is heartening that there's more medical help available today than ever before. But it's also kind of disturbing.

I went to a lecture earlier this fall, at a twenty-fifth floor Upper West Side Manhattan apartment with a stunning downtown view, sponsored by a women's networking group called 85 Broads, so named because it began as a cadre of Goldman Sachs employees, which was then headquartered at 85 Broad St. in Manhattan. It's a brash and powerful group, as the name suggests, and that night about forty of them were raptly intent on absorbing as much information as possible about the evening's topic: the red-hot science of egg freezing.

Over wine and cheese, we listened to Dr. Alan Copperman, the director of the division of reproductive endocrinology at Mount Sinai Medical Center, talk about "reproductive aging."

"Human reproduction stinks," Copperman said. "We're just not that good."

And getting less good by the minute: There's a precipitous drop in fertility in your midthirties. A thirty-five-year-old's chances of getting pregnant in a single cycle? Only 15 to 20 percent, we learned. Then there are the ever-diminishing odds of carrying a baby to term—most miscarriages are chromosomal, Copperman told us, and most chromosomal abnormalities are age-related.

Questions rained down on him like artillery fire.

"What are the chances when you're thirty-three?"

"What should I be doing at age thirty-one?"

"But can you tell us exactly when our fertility will drop off? Exactly?"

There were no precise answers, only statistics and more statistics. And then the scariest fact of the evening, one that I've seen quoted other places: When you're twenty-one years old, 90 percent of your eggs are normal. When you're forty-one, 90 percent of your eggs are abnormal.

"Over age forty-six, there has never been a baby born from a woman's own egg," Copperman announced.

But the keyword in that sentence is "egg," not "woman." Enter the sponsor and star of the evening, Extend Fertility, one company that offers a chance to stop the clock. Of course, it's not cheap or risk-free. And it's not for everybody. At the moment, age forty is the absolute maximum for egg freezing.

These women, many of whom appeared to be hovering around that cutoff, were clearly accustomed to looking for loopholes.

"But if someone comes in, and says they're thirty-five—do you ask for a birth certificate?"

"Is it possible to go overseas to have the treatment?"

The company representatives, and Copperman, did their best to make it clear, over and over again, that this technology is not a panacea. Individual results may vary.

"If a thirty-six-year-old wanted to freeze her eggs, how good are her chances?" asked one woman, her voice wavering. Then she gathered her face into a smile. "I mean, what's the return on capital employed?"

The crowd laughed, but barely.

The answer, for that thirty-six-year-old—considered by the profession to be of "AMA," or "advanced maternal age"—was, Well, it just depends.

I looked around the room and scanned the clusters of tight, solemn faces, framed by expertly highlighted hair and big diamond stud earrings. Manicured fingers scribbled furious notes. I felt like I was watching a Lifetime movie.

Near the end of the evening, the deluge of questions slowed to a drip, alternating with bursts of outrage.

"Why didn't my gynecologist tell me any of this?" said one woman, throwing up her hands.

A mere twenty-nine years old, I started to feel like an interloper. I put away my notebook, nodded to my hosts, and slipped out the door. Sliding down twenty-five floors in the silent elevator and walking out into the cold, calm night, I felt really sad for these women, creeped out by what I had just witnessed—in so much of medicine, especially the frontiers of research, there's a fine line between the public interest and public relations—and, frankly, lucky as hell. Because I think that I'm at the very tail end of the group of women who're getting gobsmacked by the fact that their fertility isn't quite the renewable resource all the forty-year-old-plus celebrity pregnancies they read about in *US Weekly* led them to believe. Or, depending on how you look at it, I'm in the vanguard of a group of women who're making somewhat different life choices because they're all too aware of that fact.

A friend from college, who graduated two years behind me, told such a drastically different version of her five-year reunion than what I recalled from mine that I had a hard time believing that we had gone to the same school. Nearly everyone, she said, was pregnant. In fact, I can't remember a single pregnant class-mate from my ten-year reunion. This same woman has friends—much younger than me—who already have consulted fertility doctors.

At the risk of sounding callous, I'll say that I think that's a little ridiculous. But I can relate to the fear that you won't be able to deliver the goods. Especially now that Jonathan and I have outed ourselves as wannabe breeders (simply by not vehe-mently claming anything to the contrary), and brought other people's hopes into the mix.

I know all four of our parents have dared to begin imagin-ing themselves as grandparents, though his are more vocal about it. Most of the comments happen when we're with Jonathan's cousin and his wife and their baby daughter, Sydney. I try to smile every time someone says something to one of us, but I can't help but thinking, *Boy, I hope I don't disappoint you!*

My newfound knowledge of how invasive it can feel to have people comment about such things, along with the fallout from a few gaffes I've made or observed along the way, brought about a new policy of mine, one which applies to all but the closest of friends: Never, ever ask any questions about fertility, pregnan-cy, or childbirth. If they want you to know, they'll volunteer the information. Not everybody who's trying to get pregnant these days finds it's as easy as falling off a log. And though it may be out of fashion in this baby-crazed age, not all married couples want children!

But for my money, creating a family made up of parents (of any gender) and children (biological by any means, or adopted) is the best reason to get married today. I know that children don't equal happiness, and that your relationship will never be the same once you have them. (Observe new parents, and you may notice that they barely even look at each other. They just pass the baby back and forth between them, and look at it.) But why else tie yourself down, unless you're building a foundation for something? Why make such a colossal promise, and extract one in return, unless you're forming a partnership to care for something that can't take care of itself?

It's also the best reason to make damn sure that marriage works. Because I automatically put kids in the picture, I'm even more awed by the magnitude of the commitment we're going to make. When I think about children, and only then, I'm afraid of divorce.

I get no comfort from statistics. I could easily tell myself that in a time when 50 percent of marriages break up, Jonathan and I can't possibly be sure how this is going to work out. I do hear people say that—about my marriage, their own, anybody's, really—offhandedly, and all the time, as if divorce were lightning strikes on the rise.

And of course I don't know exactly what it will entail, this lifetime commitment thing. Who does? But I do know that I *can* do it. If I can make it through this engagement process, doing all the right kinds of thinking and investigating along the way, and show up on May 20 with peace in my heart about what I am about to do, I can promise to stay married to Jonathan until one of us dies. And unless something goes horribly wrong along the way, I can, and will, keep my promise.

The fact that both our pairs of parents have celebrated more than thirty years of marriage helps my confidence levels. The fact that my mom is a social worker and family therapist, and sees the fallout from broken families every day, steels my resolve.

I've expressed some fears to both my mom and my future mother-in-law about how hard being a good parent seems to be. They've each been helpful. With Jonathan's mom, Lynn, it came up when we were discussing . . . how shall I put this . . . gruesome murders. We all love to joke about how Akron, their hometown, is a hotbed of blood-curdling crime. For example, Jeffrey Dahmer lived there for a time, and so did a man named Henry Heepe (pronounced "Hee-Pee"), who went to school with Lynn, lived one block away from the Cohen family home, and—no joke—killed, cooked, and ate his own mother.

This sparked a debate on the old nature/nurture conundrum. We marveled at how badly some parents can screw up. Or is it just that life can go dreadfully off kilter, despite one's best efforts? Lynn gave a little maternal shudder, thinking of poor Mrs. Dahmer, and especially Mrs. Heepe. "I was so naive when I had kids," Lynn said, laughing incredulously. "It never even occurred to me that anything could go wrong!"

Her attitude—optimism, even blissful ignorance—is looking to me like a good way to navigate the minefield of marriage and parenting without having a nervous breakdown.

My own mother was rather more clinical about it. She loaned me a copy of *The Unexpected Legacy of Divorce*, the grim findings of a twenty-five-year study begun in the '70s by researcher Judith Wallerstein, who determined that kids of divorce never entirely bounce back. But her anecdotal response was actually quite reassuring: "As long as you make your children your first priority, nothing else really matters. You can't screw up too badly as long as you do that."

Like all sage advice, though, that's a bit of a koan. Unless your marriage is a battleground of the most heinous sort, keeping it intact would be a key to making the kids your first priority, and to making sure they know that's the case. Or maybe if you make your marriage your first priority, all good things flow from that? I still haven't untangled it all in my head.

In the meantime, I've had a lot of other interesting divorce stories to chew on. First, there's the movie *The Squid and the Whale,* which I loved, though it gutted me. My friends who experienced divorce growing up thought it was way too real and raw to be considered entertainment. If you haven't lived through a divorce yourself, they say, see it, and you'll have a decent idea what it's like.

Then there's the book *Between Two Worlds* by Elizabeth Marquardt, based on another, newer study of children of divorce, this one more intimate. It backs up Wallerstein's findings, making a most convincing argument that a divorce really does rock a child's foundation, and change him or her forever. Not that kids can't recover, and be as OK as anyone else, in the big scheme of things. But reading these people's stories makes getting a divorce—and even getting married and having the kid in the first place—look unbelievably selfish.

"Selfish" just about sums it up, though. It's selfish in a macro sense to think that your exquisite DNA deserves to live on. It's selfish in a micro sense to try to plan conception to the most-convenient minute. It's certainly selfish to have a big ol' wedding, like we're having, and even more so to spend all this damn time thinking and writing about it.

But if the modern wedding is the apotheosis of a certain kind of self-absorption, maybe it makes sense that starting a family quickly follows, to even things out. Not too long from now, I know I'll be ready to add some new perspectives to my life: that of a mother, and, by extension, that of a child. We're just starting to attend the occasional group social event—bar-beque, bowling party—that feels a little empty. Here we are, a bunch of adults standing around a video arcade, or taking the ferry to a picnic lunch, and you can visualize how much more fun it would be with a kid or two on hand. You can almost see the thought bubbles over our married friends' heads.

Something else happened recently that helped me realize, despite my many anxieties and fears, how nearly ready I really am. An acquaintance of mine, a very good, smart, talented person who happens to look a bit like me (only prettier) asked if I would sell her some of my eggs. The question, posed over e-mail, took my breath away. I'd never been faced with such an ethical dilemma. Sure, we had the ads seeking donors in our college newspaper, and I would read them, and they would make me feel all kinds of things, though never remotely tempted to respond. But this was no anonymous request.

I knew almost instantly that my answer was "Sorry." Then I started trying to parse out why. In the end, it came down to money, and love. I would never sell my eggs. I would give them away, to a close family member or friend. Then, there'd be no question. If I loved the parent, then I'd love the child, too, and hopefully know it well, whether or not anyone ever knew that I was the biological parent. But when we're talking about someone far enough removed that they feel a need to offer money, or if financial gain played into my decision in any way, it just wouldn't feel right.

And there was one more thing—something I was startled to realize, and something this woman had to instinctively understand. I'm engaged now, and getting married. It's official: Soon, I'll need those eggs myself.

F WORDS OF WISDOM

If you're raring to have kids, by all means, have 'em—even before you actually get married, if "going Hollywood," as it's been called, is your style. But do keep Barry McCarthy's recommendation in mind: Ideally, you'd take two years for just you two before the birth of the child. (The engagement year counts.) If you don't take that time, just be aware that your relationship may need extra attention and care.

~

To smoothly sidestep the inevitable nosy questions, talk to your partner and establish the party line, then stick to it. Then remember how it feels to be asked a lot of nosy questions, and don't subject other people to them!

~

If kids are a sore subject for the two of you because you have different levels of interest in parenting, or if it's something you haven't yet discussed, you may want to consider slowing down the wedding planning. You absolutely must state to each other your needs and expectations on this topic before you wed.

~

Don't marry someone assuming that his or her views on having kids will change—that's a recipe for heartbreak. It's not that you shouldn't marry if you're not sure you want kids, rather, your expectations need to match. If you both know you want them, great. If you both know you don't, also great. Even if you're both unsure, great. You'll figure it out together. But if one of you is positive you do and the other is positive you don't, neither of you should expect the other to change.

November 2

THE BATTLE OF THE BOXES

How two cardboard boxes took conflict to a whole new level.

WASTEBASKETS, ladders, driving in Canada (in the pelting rain), the bathtub, parents, movies, music, health insurance, mortgages (theoretical), rent increases (real), whether I do or do not know the best way to roast a free-range chicken, and cardboard boxes. This is just a small sampling of things Jonathan and I have fought about since we decided to get married.

I can't think of a single significant fight from before we got engaged. But after our engagement (curiously, a word also defined as "a hostile encounter between military forces"), we promptly started butting heads. It was pretty much instantaneous. For a long time, one of our favorite things to fight about were two 2 x 2 x 4 cardboard boxes. When I first moved in with him, these two neatly sealed beauties were indistinguishable from all the other boxes and garbage bags and piles of crap I had sloppily moved with me from Brooklyn and strewn about the tiny apartment.

But bit by bit I found places to put all that crap, and cajoled

Jonathan into parting with some college-era home furnishings to make a little more space, and painted the bathroom and hung some pictures and reorganized the kitchen. The outline of our home began to emerge. Against that cleaner canvas, the boxes stood out once more. "When are we getting rid of these, again?" I asked him.

There was a story there, to which I had half-listened, the way one does when in preemptive, argument-winning mode: scanning for ammo; rehearsing a rebuttal. Their contents belonged to someone else, someone who lived somewhere in Indiana, and though Jonathan wanted to send them on their way, he could not, because he needed a shipping address, and the guy he wanted to ship them to, who was a struggling musician—and you know how that goes—wasn't responding to his e-mails. Or something.

All I really knew was that they did not belong to Jonathan, or to me, yet they were taking up space in our microscopic kitchen, and I wanted them gone.

I raised the topic a couple times a week, in various ways.

"Can I help you find a way to get these shipped?"

"Any news from the guy these boxes belong to?"

"Oof, my toe. When are these boxes getting out of here, again?"

"We are *not* a storage unit."

Periodically, it would hit me: Oh my God, I'm *nagging*. I'm not even married yet and I'm already a wife.

> Periodically, it would hit me: Oh my
> God, I'm *nagging*. I'm not even married
> yet and I'm already a wife.

So then I'd force myself to be nonchalant about it for a while, and try to ignore the anxiety I'd feel whenever I'd look at the boxes, focusing instead on the things Jonathan was doing *right* as we patched our home lives together. But the anxiety was still there, brewing and stewing and gathering a wicked head of steam, and every so often, Old Furious would blow.

"If these aren't out of here by the time the girls come over for brunch next month, I am personally going to drag them down to the East River and throw them in!"

So now I was nagging *and* threatening.

Still, the boxes were unmoved.

And whether I was fighting with Jonathan about them, or some other matter, I began to experience something I've come to call "emotional compounding." (If I've stolen some psychologist's copyrighted phrase, sorry—unintentional.) I'd be upset about something and so I'd pick a fight (or would it pick me?), and then I'd get smacked with a wave of negative emotions about the fact that we were fighting.

I usually don't shirk fights—I can see the value in fighting with people I love. If you don't fight from time to time, you probably don't care. (Or you're a doormat.) But these fights with Jonathan were (and, sometimes, still are) different. They make me scared: *Oh no, there's something wrong with us. This never happened before, so why is it happening now, when we're supposed to be so happy about taking this big step together?* Or frustrated: *If we can't handle these little things now, when our lives are relatively uncomplicated, how will we ever handle them?* Or sad: *Does this means that the "honeymoon" phase of our relationship is over?* Mostly, I get angry at myself for letting the fight erupt in the first place: *You're ruining what's supposed to be one of the most precious times of your life.*

I'm still working out exactly why our fighting has escalated. Have we taken the gloves off because we know the other person will be sticking around, and so now we feel freer to ask for, even do battle for, the things we need—not to mention reveal things and exhibit behaviors we were previously inclined to conceal? Are we blowing up issues that might have receded into the background before the engagement because we now know that whatever it is we're fighting about might be an issue *for the rest of our lives*—and that's a long time to put up with something? Certainly, the stakes are higher, and that's making us twitchier. And because we're living together for the first time, we're suddenly more susceptible to each other's moods, each of us more apt to let our own outlook be colored by the other's momentary (or longer) depression or frustration; more apt to get caught in a feedback loop that's tough to break. And, of course, when you're got a negative internal monologue going on, most forecasts look dark: *What if this means we're not meant to be?*

But when I stop panicking and look around, I do see evidence of the engagement period being rough for other people, too. Again, I go back to the Smart Marriages conference, and remember what Barry McCarthy said about fighting early on being good for cementing your bond. (Though that's harder to believe when you're in the midst of it than when you're taking notes at a lecture!) I remember that scene in *Father of the Bride* when Kimberly Williams's Annie Banks calls off the wedding because her fiancé buys her a blender for her birthday—and she's positive that means he now sees her as the little wife in the kitchen. (Everything is a bit more fraught with meaning these days, it's true.)

I've found a couple books that have made me feel better, too, including *Emotionally Engaged: A Bride's Guide to Surviving the "Happiest" Time of Her Life.* The author, Boston-area therapist Allison Moir-Smith, is a self-described "renegade wedding-industry person." When I read the phrase "Most brides-to-be tell me that during their engagements, they fight more, have less sex, feel less close, and spend a lot of time evaluating and analyzing their relationship," I knew that I needed to get Allison's voice and ideas in *Tango,* and so we worked together on excerpting the book for an issue of the magazine.

The book resonated with me because it was born of the author's own experience with being a bride, much like another book, this one about fighting and nothing else. In *52 Fights: A Newlywed's Confession,* Jennifer Jeanne Patterson gives a week-by-week account of their spat-by-spat progress to their first anniversary.

"Oh, we fought all the time when we were engaged," Patterson told me when I called her up to talk. "For us, the engagement period was the very first time we had to work toward a goal together. Before that, you're basically just living your lives in parallel. And all of a sudden you have to bend."

The wedding wasn't the end of it for Patterson and her husband. The fighting really started freaking her out about three months into her marriage, and she responded by writing about it: "I first started to write the column when we were right in the heat of it and I wasn't sure our marriage was going to make it," she said. "I knew we were going to hang in there, but what kind of a marriage is that just to hang in there? I didn't want to float around for ten years being unhappy."

She told me that when she let her husband read her pieces, she often found that she had misinterpreted his position. "I always assumed that Matt was seeing the issue the same way I was," she said. "But he'd say 'I don't think like that,' and it would come as a big shock to know that he thought different than me, and that he expresses himself differently than I do."

She told me this back before Jonathan and I moved in together, and at the time I thought it was a fairly simpleminded comment. *A "big shock"? Of course he thinks differently, communicates differently—you're not conjoined twins.*

And wouldn't chronic fighting stem from something more complex, more insidious, than the immutable fact that the two halves of a couple, by definition, occupy separate brains and bodies?

Not too long after that interview, those boxes entered my life.

And it wasn't too long after my chuck-them-in-the-East

River comment that Jonathan and I went to the first of the three marriage education courses we're scheduled to take. This class was called "Relationship Enhancement," and it consisted of two days in a shabby, overheated basement office in Bethesda, Maryland, with three other couples and two sweet, grandmotherly facilitators who taught us communication skills, specifically empathic listening.

Empathic listening is not merely "active" listening, or parroting back what your partner says to make sure that you heard them correctly. It's becoming a giant, empty ear; listening with your whole body, brain, and intuition so you become a vessel into which your partner's thoughts—and, more importantly, feelings—can flow. You try to have empathy: *The action of understanding, being aware of, being sensitive to, and vicariously experiencing the feelings, thoughts, and experience of another* (Webster's). When you think you've got it, you repeat it back to them, and they either say "Yes, that's it," or "No, that's not quite it, it's more like *this*," and then you try again and it keeps going back and forth until your partner is confident that you understand the essence of his or her feelings about a particular matter. The beauty of the process is that the listener helps the speaker to gradually clarify his or her own point of view, so *both* parties begin to understand that behind someone's vehement position there might be a feeling, and maybe then an important or particularly painful memory, and then, perhaps, another feeling, and another, and another still.

Like peeling an onion.

With practice, you can engage your intuition more fully,

making small leaps to try to tease out the feelings behind your partner's words more quickly. With each success, your partner trusts you more, and, as a result gives you more information about him or herself, stuff you didn't even know you didn't know. It's a virtuous cycle.

You can get startlingly raw startlingly fast, but though there's risk there, it feels controlled, safe. That's partly because "dialoguing"—the "Relationship Enhancement" name and process for employing the empathic listening technique—is very specific and measured and you have to take turns. And you can't interrupt. As a result, it's a great way to address a point of contention without either partner hitting the roof or getting distracted by other issues.

So after a good amount of practicing on various nit-picky things in that overheated basement, we were sent off to a late breakfast with the goal of doing a dialogue about a more loaded issue in our relationship.

At the Original Pancake House, over a gooey apple pancake and crisp, salty hash browns, amid noisy tables full of suburban teenagers in Juicy Couture sweatpants, I learned what was in the boxes. Up to that point, somehow, I'd never asked about their contents. And Jonathan had never told me that they contained several thousand dollars worth of CDs; copies of a record by a favorite band from college in Bloomington, Indiana, the only album ever released on an independent record label he had started with some friends. The CDs are all that's left from the venture; they're the joint property of Jonathan, his two partners, and the artists; and while the financial aspects of it are quite complex, the bottom line is simple: The inventory didn't move, and everyone lost a lot of money.

With the help of the "dialogue," Jonathan supplied those facts, and then he filled in the feelings: Getting rid of those boxes meant acknowledging a failure, and saying good-bye to a dream.

And I had threatened to throw them away.

The boxes didn't mean anything to me, so of course they didn't mean anything to him, either; he knew there was no room for them in our apartment or our life as well as I did, and therefore he was being lazy, aggravating, and downright rude to me by not doing anything about it.

The realization left me speechless.

I had been callous, careless, selfish, and, worst of all, ignorant: I didn't even know what I didn't know.

After a lot of blinking and staring and, finally, on my part, apologizing, we kept going in the dialogue, and had another breakthrough: I was able to clearly articulate to him, for the first time, that clutter makes me anxious in general, and that in this particular instance his reluctance to make space in our newly shared dwelling was holding me back from relaxing and feeling like I was home. I felt petty expressing such feelings in light of what I had just learned, but Jonathan acknowledged and—I might as well plunge into jargon here—"validated" my concerns, and said he wanted to address the problem.

Plus, he told me, he knew the record label was over, and that it was time to say good-bye, to make space for other things.

We didn't work out a plan for what to do about the boxes

right away, but we understood each other a lot better immediately, and quite powerfully. And when we got back home from that weekend, the sight of those boxes didn't make me grit my teeth anymore. I didn't begrudge them their cubic footage. Now there were two of us invested in making sure that they were safely delivered to the proper place, no matter how long it took.

And in the weird way that life takes care of things when you stop trying to master them, the boxes disappeared in a matter of weeks—not in time for the brunch, but sooner than I'd ever hoped to imagine they would. Jonathan got in touch with a guy in the Bloomington music scene, who, coincidentally, was having a festival at which this band was going to perform. The record hadn't been available for purchase in three years, but with our help a new shipment could arrive just in time to sell at the show. I printed the UPS labels myself, and stayed home from work that morning to wait for the pickup.

Now, we laugh about the boxes. It's remarkable: Because we resolved the problem by each acting out of love and care for the other person, we feel really good about something we used to bicker about. It's a mark in the "win-win" column, a relationship success, and that's a confidence booster.

And guess what: Jennifer Patterson ended up in the same place. Eventually, the fighting that once freaked her out came to seem important, cathartic, bonding—in short, vital and good. One thing that's "nice about fighting during your first year of marriage," she told me, "is that you realize that your marriage isn't going to end because you don't agree." And it helped her reach another wise conclusion: "I don't think you can change your partner," Patterson continued. "I think you need a partner who's willing to change for you. I try to be in tune with Matt's needs, and if there's something in his life or in our marriage that he needs, I don't think that can go unanswered. But it took a lot of fighting for me to realize, 'Why am I defending this position so vehemently? Does it really matter? If it's this important to him, can I change?'"

Some experts, including my hero Barry McCarthy, actually count an "engagement year" as the first year of marriage, especially if you're living together. It kind of feels that way, at times—like we're already married. The nagging, the sulking, the fighting—they're all there, and for all our attempts to use our new skills to fight well, and to gainful ends, we still blow it from time to time. I know we always will. I suppose the goal is to keep more marks in the "win-win" column than the "win-lose" column—which, where a marriage is concerned, is probably the same as the "lose-lose" column.

But no matter the outcome, we two combatants share a prize: With every skirmish, we learn more and more about each other, get more and more intimate. As I realized the other day, with shock, and then delight, the fighting is helping us become a *family*.

Just like Jennifer and Matt, who, for the record, are still together, still happy, still sparring—and now raising a son, Max, who, Jennifer told me with a laugh, provides all kinds of new things to fight about.

F WORDS OF WISDOM

Don't freak out if you're fighting. Everybody does, even if nobody admits it. And it only can provide opportunities for the two of you to get closer.

~

Remember that your partner doesn't exist to annoy you. Sometimes it feels that way, but it's not all about you. If you can find a way to figure out how he sees the situation, you might learn something extremely surprising.

~

If you can stomach the cheese factor, try the "dialoguing" process described in this piece. It's a miracle-worker, though you have to see it in action to believe it. A Google search for "empathic listening" turns up a few good articles that can give you more background.

November 29

HOT FOR CLASSMATE

Marriage education classes make a good infidelity insurance policy—even when they teach you what not to do.

L ET ME JUST SAY it now and get it over with: Someone I met in a marriage ed class asked me out.

Yes, a fellow student.

Who was there with his girlfriend.

It was actually a broader "relationship ed" class, not specifically for engaged or married couples, but everyone in the room was part of a couple, and sitting next to the other half of that couple, and if they weren't married or planning to be, they were serious enough about each other to spend fourteen hours in a drab hotel conference room learning how to make their relationship better.

Ostensibly.

The class was on a weekend, and I got the e-mail the following Thursday. He had "told himself he wouldn't contact me," but, ultimately, "you just never know," and, therefore, he decided to write to find out if the attraction was mutual. "Please button this up and keep it to yourself!" he wrote; half plea, half command. Then he proceeded to tell me that he had read my columns, and liked my writing.

I'm still not sure if he's really that dim, or merely self-destructive. And why he thought I might be willing to meet him for a clandestine coffee/sangria/elopement is also a mystery. Turns out we sat near each other on the second day of the class—I pieced that much together later—but when I first read his e-mail, I had no idea who he was. In fact, I needed my Jonathan's help to figure it out.

I forwarded the e-mail to him immediately, mainly so we could marvel at and laugh about it together, but also to keep my conscience totally clear. But his cool, amused-as-I-was reaction reassured me of his trust in me, and his confidence in himself, and it gave me a fillip of joy at being part of a relationship properly calibrated, healthily close.

But not long after I got that e-mail, I chatted with Diane Sollee, director of the Coalition for Marriage, Family and Couples Education, who has been an invaluable resource and cheerleader throughout our (rather long, as you can tell) marriage ed process. Because the incident was fresh in my mind, I cautiously told Sollee what had happened, expecting her to be scandalized. Instead, she laughed. "That's such good practice for marriage!" she exclaimed, and proceeded to tell me about the people who would full-on proposition her when she was married. People who not only knew she was taken, but also knew her husband—quite well. People whom she swears she never so much as glanced at in that way, and I believe her.

I'm not the most naive girl on the planet, but that conversation got under my skin. Are people really that cavalier about commitment, that brash about their own desires? Are threats to fidelity and monogamy truly everywhere—even at relationship seminars?

It does seem, at the moment, that an American fiancé is in a dicey spot. Did you happen to see *The Family Stone*, *Rumor Has It*, *Match Point*, *Brokeback Mountain*, or *Imagine Me and You*? Even a novel I read recently, *London Is the Best City in America*, is about fleeing fiancés, and, in one way or another, ties back to wanting someone you're not about to wed. Are broken engagements the new starter marriages?

Whether that's truly the zeitgeist, or just my own prewedding vulnerability talking, I do feel—now, more than ever—that the forty hours we spent in class together was time well invested.

Here's the basic premise: Nobody gets married with the goal of being miserable, or having an affair, or of eventually getting divorced. People get married because they're in love and they make each other happy and so they want to be together. So what goes wrong? Whatever ultimately ends a marriage—cheating, many times, or those elusive "irreconcilable differences"—it's likely the fruit of one or both parties simply growing disgusted with the mess they've made, and deciding to look for greener pastures elsewhere. So marriage education gives you the tools to get closer, relate better, and clean up the mess, to make your home a place you want to live in again. Or, in the case of people who aren't married yet, to prevent the mess from accumulating in the first place.

You and your intended and a bunch of strangers sit around and talk, learning about the building blocks of good relationships and practicing communication skills on one another, in the name of acquiring tools that will help you keep your relationship shipshape, and minimize the desire to stray.

If you think that smacks of group therapy, you're not far off. Not for you, right? But wait—let me quote Reese Witherspoon, in *Interview* magazine, on her reaction to the tabloid frenzy at the news that she and hubby Ryan Philippe were in couples' counseling: "I think if anybody rests on the idea that they are perfect or their life is perfect or their relationship is perfect and is so troubled about destroying the facade as opposed to getting what's real, that is troublesome. Who is so arrogant and vain that they don't want people to know they're real or human. That they're fallible?"

Right on, Reese.

A little background: The field originally called "psycho-education" evolved in the mid-'60s, when a few academics— Bernard Guerney of Penn State, and David Olsen and Sherod Miller of the University of Minnesota—developed some concrete ideas about how couples could treat each other better. Their goal was to share this information with couples before things got too complicated, Sollee explains: "They thought, 'Why do we need to wait for therapy, which people don't go to, anyway—the logic goes 'I'm not crazy, I just don't love you'— to get people this information?"

But, for a variety of reasons, these ideas and workshops were relatively unknown outside of therapy circles about a decade ago. But the field is still very fragmented, and virtually unheard of by anyone who doesn't work in it, or hasn't come upon it by chance, or dire necessity.

And it's definitely got an image problem.

I of all people—an editor at a magazine about relationships and a fiancé at the same time—should be into the idea. But I was very apprehensive before our first workshop. Was it going to be hopelessly cheesy, unrealistically hopeful, overly simplistic? An utter waste of time? Or what if it was scary, and took us places we didn't want to go? Was it possible that we could walk away from the weekend liking each other less, instead of more? What was I pulling Jonathan into?

The morning of the first seminar, the aforementioned "Relationship Enhancement," he looked dazed; I'm sure I did, too. We both were dragging our feet. We had stayed out too late the night before, and drank too much, and were silent and crabby on the journey to the class. If I hadn't been on assignment, I'm not sure we wouldn't have played hooky.

But we showed up, sat down, and started listening. Though I liked the class's premise immediately—acknowledging that "life is a manipulation," and suggesting we learn to manipulate respectfully, compassionately—it still took me a while to drop my guard. At first, I was afraid that I was in for a *Clockwork Orange*-esque deprogramming session, and I was loathe to have my tools blunted, most of all the wit I've honed to help me get my way in life. Did it really need to be filed down in service to my new status as half of a couple? To be a good partner, must I be boiled down into verbal and emotional oatmeal?

But slowly, willingly, I started to soften, and by the end of the course (well, you read the last chapter) we learned how to actually make progress rather than rehashing the same old issues again and again, and how to turn scary things, annoying things—anything, really—into an opportunity to "bond." "Good marriages are held together by vulnerability and dialogue," said one of the facilitators. "That is like cement that holds people together. Not wanting to get vulnerable, to get down to where we live, is what breaks up marriages."

It's an interesting way to look at it—that relationships might rupture because people are afraid to lay themselves bare, really let someone in, show them why they are angry, or hurting, and let them help. It starts with believing that the other person truly wants to help, not to make your life miserable. But it's scary to let them, especially because the closer you get to someone, the more power you cede. "It's not hard to figure out how to hurt someone," said the other facilitator. "The more you know about them, the more you love them, the easier it is to hurt them." (And it's so true. Sometimes something pops out of my mouth during an argument with Jonathan that makes me feel as if I've slapped a child.)

In short, the class taught me that you have to be willing and able to "go there" with another person. It's often so hard to "go there" by yourself that bringing someone else along seems near-ly impossible. But the "skills" they taught us that day, along with other simple nuggets of wisdom—that "try" is a word that you should excise from your vocabulary because it allows too much room for defeat; that in any argument with your partner, only 20 percent is between the two of you, and the rest is about your history, which, much of the time, is unknown by your partner; that simply having a shared calendar on the fridge helps enormously; that there's an Irish tradition of gifting newly-weds with a "make-up bell" that one person rings when they're ready to end an argument—made it all seem a bit easier.

And it brought home the obvious, but easy-to-forget-during-an-engagement fact that we aren't the only people on the planet who'll have marital issues. Everyone does.

Our classmates—all married, all different—underscored that fact. We learned as much from them and their back-stories and their challenges and the way they treated each other in the presence of near-strangers as we did from the facilitators. At the end of the second exhausting day, I watched one woman look into the eyes of her husband and father of her two children, say "you're a good man," then kiss him on the lips. Could we ask for better inspiration?

> We aren't the only people on the planet who'll have marital issues. Everyone does.

Our rosy glow faded a bit, however, when we sat down to do our prework for the next class, Marriage Success Training. We griped about the complicated instructions for completing "RE-

LATE," an online compatibility "inventory" with—in my opinion—an attitude problem. (The copy on the Web site includes such choices phrases as "So, you think you're in love?")

RELATE (like similar inventories, such as PREPARE and FOCCUS) is designed "to evaluate the quality of a relationship." Aren't you pleased that someone has created an objective measure for that? No more sleepless nights! But seriously, it's a helpful tool, if you take it somewhat lightly. And, of course, read the disclaimers: "While there are no known risks involved in completing RELATE, a few of the questions may trigger some discomforting memories."

Perhaps you can see why Jonathan and I took to mocking the inventory, à la that old *Saturday Night Live* "Happy Fun Ball" bit ("Do not taunt Happy Fun Ball!" "If Happy Fun Ball begins to smoke, get away immediately. Seek shelter and cover head."), and why we felt more relief than anything else when the bar graphs that charted our personality characteristics, values, family backgrounds, and relationship experiences revealed no truly alarming discrepancies.

After all that buildup, the seminar itself was much better than we had feared. The facilitators, married couple Greg and Patty Kuhlman, were very cool, and very frank. They created the curriculum themselves, and the whole tone was hipper than Relationship Enhancement. Plus, they weren't afraid to share anecdotes from their own marriage. ("We observe the three-foot rule. When she throws the Kleenex box, it can't come within three feet of me.")

They had lots of data for us—facts and figures and time-

tested suggestions for solving widespread marital problems—
and we took notes. It was a kind of survey course of the last
decade or so of research into why marriages work, or don't. It
also took the infidelity bull by the horns: Turns out that the risk
of cheating is the highest in the first two years of marriage,
"when your bond is not yet cemented enough to handle the
challenges you face." (There's that b-word again. And that sta-
tistic surprised everyone in the class: When Greg polled the
room about when they thought infidelity rates were highest,
most people said "seven years in" or "after the birth of a child."
No one, including Jonathan and me, had considered that the
early years could be toughest.)

They talked a lot about sex in general, and about its role as
the "glue" in a relationship, but above all else wanted us to
absorb what they called "the big three":

1. Keep your 5:1 ratio up; a mantra based on John Gottman's
    research findings that you need five positive interac-
    tions to balance the impact of one negative interaction.
2. Make time for each other every day, and protect your
    relationship from other people—including your chil-
    dren, if and when you have them.
3. Avoid unrealistically expecting your partner to change.
    Change some of your own behavior first.

It was mostly common sense, and there was a bit too much
gender stereotyping for our taste, but overall it was a very solid
course, packed full of good information.

The last course we took, called PAIRS (Practical Skills for Emotional Literacy), was facilitated by a lovely woman named Carolyn Perla, and was the weekend version of what is typically a 120-hour class. It was more similar to Relationship Enhancement than Marriage Success Training, though it incorporated elements of the latter, too. (There was no inventory component, however.) Of all the facilitators, Perla was the most straightforward about why we were there ("I want to tell you right now that unconditional love does not exist") and the most realistic about how her students might be feeling about the class. "Some of this can seem a little hokey, but I ask you to suspend your judgment," she said early on the first day.

Perla gave us the clearest definition of, yep, "bonding," describing it as "emotional closeness and physical closeness at the same time." She was careful to point out that "you can have sex without bonding, and vice versa," and, even more interestingly, that "many people who think they need sex actually need bonding."

Hmmm. That makes sense. Sex is everywhere, but really connecting with someone is rare. When it happens, you've hit the good stuff, the stuff you'd never dream of leaving. And if it's not happening, well, maybe that's when you roam.

After a whole workweek's worth of hours in the classroom—some of which, I'll admit, found me feeling panicky, trapped, and positive my precious time could be better spent elsewhere—I've reached a few conclusions. One, of course, is that not everyone who attends them is seriously focused on improving their current relationship. Two is that I do think that classes like these are worthwhile. Jonathan and I couldn't help but "bond" a little more with every class, and that alone is worth the time and money. Three is that I recommend taking both an inventory and a communication skills class like R.E. or PAIRS. Four is that I'm glad we took a communication skills class first.

When we had completed the last course, I asked Diane Sollee if she thought order mattered. "Oh, yes," she told me over the phone, "Bernie Guerney and the rest looked at the inventory idea and decided that it's dangerous. You could break up a couple that's going to have the next Abraham Lincoln or Albert Einstein! I know couples who have broken up after going through the inventory—you send them into it without the skills to talk empathetically and you can have all kinds of trouble."

I guess I should have asked that question sooner. It was pure luck that we took the classes in the order that we did. And that's emblematic of another conclusion I've come to about marriage education: It's still a bit too haphazard for my taste. There's no one class I would unequivocally send my best friends to, or recommend to my younger brother. The best classes aren't available nationwide. Someone needs to create something more accessible, more affordable, and more appealing than the options currently available; a one-size-fits-most class that your average-to-somewhat-enlightened engaged couple could actually see themselves taking. And then they need to market the hell out of it, so that couple can easily find it.

Still, this has been quite a time of self-discovery for both

Jonathan and me, and of discovery about what, at *Tango*, we like to call "the art of being together" in a world full of distractions. Did we take these classes because we were tempted to cheat? Not even close. In fact, before my marriage ed experience, it never occurred to me that someone else could pose a threat to our relationship—I thought it much more likely that we'd be our own undoing, bring it down from the inside. I still think that's true, but I also have a much wider perspective on what making a commitment to someone entails, from seeing, up close and in a tell-almost-all environment, other people who are doing just that—or not. I walked away from these classes with a much more realistic view of how fragile a relationship really is. Never mind the *scary* statistics, such as the "60 percent of people in marriages will be unfaithful" that the Kuhlmans quoted. Real-life examples are even more revealing. When you work in a group, as Diane Sollee put it, "You really see how stupid people are, how obnoxious and dense and mean. You can't see it so much when it's just the two of you."

Ideally, we'd faithfully, systematically practice everything we learned—the better we are at being good to one another, the better inoculated we are against potential threats like Mr. Email. But I'm satisfied that we retained at least a bit of it, and now we know it's there if we need it. Maybe we'll take another class later in life. We'll definitely hang onto the manuals and our notes, I'm sure, and someday our kids will find them while poking around the basement, and wonder what life was like back when their mom and dad were, impossibly, young . . . and attractive enough to be hit on.

F Words of Wisdom

Hopefully, infidelity is the last thing on your mind while you're engaged. But that doesn't mean that threats aren't out there. Your engagement is a good time to take preventative measures to thwart them.

~

Get as much premarital education as you can schedule, and stomach. Marriage-ed advocate Carolyn Washburn, of the Utah State University Washington County Extension Office, puts it in perspective with these thoughts about the current marriage-license policy in her state: "To obtain a license to be a cosmetologist, you need one thousand hours of hair-cutting experience. You need five hundred hours minimum of education to be a massage therapist. However, zero hours of education are needed to obtain a marriage license."

~

There are many, many different kinds of marriage education courses out there for the taking. To search a directory of programs by state, go to www.smartmarriages.com/search.html.

Here's the scoop on the three classes mentioned in this chapter:

Relationship Enhancement: Currently available only in the D.C. area; $350 per couple. If you are able to travel to attend the seminar, it's worth it. www.nire.org

MST: Available in the New York, D.C., Philadelphia, Boston, Chicago, and Miami metro areas; $450–$500 per couple. www.stayhitched.com

PAIRS: Educators get trained to teach this curriculum, then run workshops wherever they want, so availability is wider. Prices vary. www.pairs.com

Many of the existing marriage education classes are not cheap. Ask for one as a gift from someone who cares about the future of your union. And no, whatever your church or temple has cooked up for you is probably not enough. According to Diane Sollee, until seven or eight years ago, that kind of marriage prep wasn't "skill-based" at all, but was solely about pep talks on being sure you really love each other enough, knowing it's going to take commitment through the rough patches, and, of course, faith in God, which was put forth as the crucial glue that holds it all together. Many religious groups are beginning to teach skills and conflict management in their standard premarriage workshops, but for the time being, it's still advisable to sign up for an independent course as well.

~

If you can't find a class you like in your area, or travel to attend something good, at the very least you should take an online inventory, and/or get some coaching from afar. www.premaritalonline.com is a good source for customized marriage preparation—options include online/self-directed ($189) or phone/video conferencing ($379), and they have an in-person option as well ($379). Diane Sollee also recommends a service called Marriage Preparation by Long Distance (www.trudycosta.com), and offers a full list of online inventories at www.smartmarriages.com/directory_browse.html#

inventories. EHarmony.com also offers a $75 questionnaire and computer-generated analysis of your relationship, including a profile that points out strengths and possible problem areas. You can add on a series of instructional videos to bring the total to $239.

~

Investigate the steps involved in getting your marriage license as soon as you know when and where you're getting married—and check to see if your state offers a discount to couples who have completed a premarital ed program. Several states, including Florida, Maryland, Minnesota, Oklahoma, and Tennessee, do, and others should follow suit as more and more legislators seek funding for these programs. Though these measures, including the $150 million of federal grant money recently earmarked for "healthy marriages and responsible fatherhood," can be highly politicized and controversial, the classes themselves really are valuable—anything that makes them more affordable and more widely available is a good thing.

December 7

MEET THE FUTURE

Even when the natives are friendly, the first meeting of your folks and his can be a feat of diplomacy.

"PARENTS' WEEKEND," as we've been calling it, has come and gone, and Jonathan has gone, too, on a business trip, and so I'm alone on the couch in mismatched socks, scarfing takeout aloo palak and naan, drinking red wine, and breathing—finally. Finally.

Not that this past weekend, when our parents met for the first time, was contentious. On the contrary, and to my great relief, it was fun. Both parties seemed to genuinely like each other, and to enjoy spending time together. But I still found it stressful, in the way a diamond in one of those tension-mount rings must feel stressed: locked into place by the pressure coming at it from both sides. For this initial meeting, at least, fitting these two different bodies of people into the same space was a squeeze—even though the "space" was as large as the island of Manhattan.

Of course, if that weren't the way of the world, *Meet the Fockers* wouldn't have grossed more than $46 million at the box office opening weekend. During his speech at the Smart Marriages conference, Bill Doherty said that "*Every* marriage is an intercultural marriage," and I think he really nailed it. Yes, our families are the same in many ways: both white and middle-class, with college-educated parents, and two kids. Both sets of parents have strong, long-lasting marriages, and similar values, primary among which is putting their kids first—a factor that has not only enabled Jonathan and me to become who we are, and to form this relationship with one another, but also should help our parents relate quite well over time.

We're even all from the Midwest—but therein lies the first difference, albeit a minor one. I grew up thinking that Nebraska was as Midwestern as you got, and was shocked to arrive at college and meet people from, among other places, Ohio (Jonathan's home state, as you know) who defined themselves that way, too. Ohio? Weren't they Easterners? Likewise, they said I wasn't from the Midwest—I was from the Plains, or the Heartland. Don't laugh—I've long since determined that, yes, the Midwest is big enough for everybody who wants to call it home. But to our families, with deep roots in their home states and lives less peripatetic than ours, what seem like small regional differences actually can take on greater significance.

And then there's the major difference: Jonathan's family is Jewish; mine, hodgepodge-Christian. So far, religion has been the elephant in the corner: obvious, of course, but well-behaved, and sitting quietly, waiting for someone to goose it—something that's bound to happen eventually.

Or perhaps not. Each of us certainly discusses religion with our own family, and we discuss it with each other, and I've even had a few tentative conversations with the Cohens. But I could see us going years before my mom brings it up with Jonathan's mom, or Jonathan's dad with my dad, or any permutation of that sort. If it even happens at all.

But even if you stick to standard conversational game— movies, work, recent travels, and, of course, the upcoming wedding—it's not really what you say, but how you say it. The little cues you give; your style of interacting with people; idioms, inside jokes, and family lore—all the stylistic, micro-cultural things that determine how much of ourselves we recognize in other people, and how much feels foreign. Before the weekend, I found myself wondering whether Jonathan's dad would get my dad's folksy sayings. And would my mom, who works full-time, understand Jonathan's stay-at-home mom's perspective?

I tried not to overthink it, though, because I know the two tribes won't have to spend a lot of time together, and possibly might not see each other that much after the wedding—if at all. Plus, their relationships with each other are a long second to our relationships with each of them, and, of course to our relationship with one another, the reason we're all here in the first place. It occurs to me that unlike "mother-in-law," or "son-in-law," there's no name for what Jonathan's parents are to my brother, or what our parents are to each other. If you can't title it, it's not really a family relationship, right?

But it is becoming more and more clear to me that they are not nothing to each other. They may inhabit two distinct worlds, but we'll pass back and forth freely between them, depositing custom and culture as we travel. We've already made several rounds since we got engaged. Trips home to Akron for family gatherings. Wedding-scouting weekends in Nebraska. Hosting each set of parents, separately, in New York. We spent almost a week with his family over Thanksgiving; and there's a week in Lincoln on the horizon, over Christmas, as well as wedding showers for me in both hometowns.

Though it wasn't really conscious, we've been equitable. The consequence has been strenuous travel for us, at a frequency that's risen precipitously since the engagement. My friend Joanne even commented on it the other day, saying, "It seems like ever since you got engaged you've been so busy, spending time with one family or another."

True, we've logged more family time than usual, for two reasons. One, the day we got engaged, we basically started functioning as a married couple. No one's made a family trip without the other's presence. That will change, I think, as we move along, but for right now we're in lockstep.

Two, we've been trying to make sure that no one comes up short. Like many of our generation, so much more mobile than our parents, we've ended up a long way from where we were raised. I suppose we won't really start feeling the full effects until later, first when there are coveted grandchildren to cuddle and spoil, and then, even more acutely, when our parents need us to help care for them.

It just isn't something you think about when you're living your life and dating and falling in love. *You're adorable, and brilliant, and you make damned good scrambled eggs, but wait—are our families geographically compatible?* For people who want to marry within a religion, or into a strong, specific cultural heritage, the lifestyle and location of their significant other's parents may matter very much. But for self-centric, urban nomad types like Jonathan and me, it's way down the list.

> You're adorable, and brilliant, and you make damned good scrambled eggs, but wait—are our families geographically compatible?

Still, it's hardly trivial. One wedding book I read said something like "It's important to make sure that your parents meet briefly before the wedding, even if it's only the night before for dinner or drinks." To me, that's lunacy. It not only smacks of disrespect for the families, but also sounds like a recipe for disaster. What couple wants their parents meeting for the first time less than 24 hours before they're legally bound together? I know not everyone has the same kind of relationships that we have with our parents, or even has their parents in their lives by the time they get married, but I think it makes sense to have the most important people—whomever they are—in your individual lives meet sooner rather than later. Jonathan felt the same way. It was very important to us that the parents meet early enough in our engagement for them to gain some level of comfort with each other, and to glimpse the other world their child would soon be sucked into. On a more practical level, I wanted them to have a context for the inevitable collaboration in the lead-up to the wedding: the rehearsal dinner, mother-of-the-bride outfits, bridal-shower coordinating.

We agonized about when and where and how to make the introduction, finally settling on a short weekend in neutral territory. We considered going someplace completely neutral, such as Chicago, since it was more geographically desirable for parents coming from Nebraska and Ohio, but ultimately decided that we preferred the symbolism of meeting in the place where Jonathan and I now live.

We also worked hard to quell our own nerves, and to avoid any awkwardness. "Let's try a new tactic, and go in pretending like these are just interesting people, not our future in-laws," I recommended to Jonathan, and to myself, trying to defuse some of the pressure. "We're both good with people, and these are just people, so what's the big deal?" We joked about making trading cards for all the players—Jonathan's brother Brian's idea—but ultimately went with short, e-mailed bios instead, just so everyone had some basic information.

So as to prevent that "too much, too soon" feeling, we also shied away from total integration. We only planned two big-group events, a Friday-night dinner and a Saturday-morning brunch. We put them up in different hotels, and more or less moved in our different camps. We mingled in cabs and at mealtimes, but each time we got together, we met and parted as two distinct families, reluctant to . . . what? To fully blend, I guess, because blending with the new also means separating from the old.

For Friday's dinner we sought a warm, familial vibe, and nothing stuffy: A low-key neighborhood Italian restaurant was the perfect solution. The next day's brunch, hosted by Jonathan's mom's first cousin, Carol, who is a fairy-godmother figure to both of us, was equally successful. She cooked, decorated with lush bouquets of white roses, and filled the house with interesting people.

Gathering in a home added a crucial element we couldn't provide ourselves, given the tiny dimensions of our apartment. I got to be guest of honor rather than hostess, and could pay more attention to everyone and how they were interacting. My parents got to see a "real New York apartment"—a Woody Allen movie-worthy place that's way closer to their idealized vision of the city than where Jonathan and I live—as well as meet more of Jonathan's family. And everybody got to relax a little. That brunch made for good mingling. Jonathan's mom told stories about his childhood to my dad. My mom leafed through an album of Jonathan's cousin's photographs. Brother Brad, who had graciously agreed to come up from Washington, D.C., to serve as a diversion, circulated like a politician. Everyone gathered for a snapshot, our first official extended family portrait, in which, bizarrely, almost everyone was wearing shades of green and blue.

So between our surrogate Italian kitchen, Carol's beautiful apartment, and Lucky Jack's, the cozy bar right across the street from our place—which I have started calling "the living room,"

> In a larger sense, each of us is a foreigner
> in this marriage thing, a foreigner who
> needs to assimilate, yet somehow remain
> true to a native land.

and which was the site for both introductions and farewells—
we made it through the weekend.

We really didn't plan to have the hellos and good-byes in a
bar, but there may have been subliminal forces at work—if any
situation calls for a drink, it's the first-time meeting of future
in-laws. Cocktails or no, both parties reported having a great
time. Of course, there were a few jokes that bombed, some
straining, and more than a little behind-the-scenes eyebrow-
raising, I'm sure. But this is no easy task. In addition to creating
our own new world as a married couple, we're learning how to
operate comfortably in each other's old worlds, and how to
merge them successfully when circumstances require.

In a larger sense, each of us is a foreigner in this marriage
thing, a foreigner who needs to assimilate, yet somehow remain
true to a native land. When we visit the "old countries," we
must be good ambassadors. And when our heads of state meet,
well, we must plan a big old party.

F Words of Wisdom

If your parents, or parentlike figures in your life, haven't yet met, plan a rendezvous, stat.

~

When you do come together, don't overschedule. Make sure everybody has some separate-family time.

~

It's wise to meet in a restaurant or other neutral location for the very first meeting. Choose something delicious, unpretentious, and quiet—many restaurants are so loud that it's hard to converse—but not too quiet. Pick a place where the other patrons seem to be having fun. Request a round table, which is ideal for six or so people: No one feels stuck in Siberia at the end.

~

If you have a couple days together, spending some time in someone's home—even if it's not yours, your parents', or your fiancé's parents—during the first visit can really help people mingle and relax.

~

Bringing siblings along can take some of the focus off the two of you.

January 4

IN SICKNESS AND IN HEALTH

Forget the first kiss—the first cold (or flu, or fever) is when you start realizing the true weight of that familiar wedding-day promise.

WITH THE PACE we've been keeping, I knew it had to happen one of these days, and finally, it did. I have a cold.

It's nothing major, just a brain-fuzzing, snot-factory, pain-in-the-ass-but-entirely-garden-variety cold. But whenever I get sick enough to have to slow down, but not so sick that I literally can't get out of bed, I spaz out. As much as I'd like to be, I'm not one of those cuddly, docile patients who curl up with the Puffs and the remote and the Luden's Honey Lemon throat drops, eliciting sympathetic coos from all who enter the room. No, I behave more or less like a caged animal. I lose perspective, despair of ever being well again, and fret over all the things that aren't getting done while I'm trapped in an out-of-service body.

My tactics—ineffectual as they may be—are my cry for sympathy and attention. *Baby me.* Does everyone regress when they have a cold? Me, I'm right back to childhood: less capable of asking for what I want, and at the same time needier, and more vulnerable.

That's why I'm feeling a little put out that Jonathan is hesitant to sleep in the same bed with me. Oh, he hasn't said as much. But I can tell. The way he gingerly flips back the duvet. Darts his eyes at me. Takes a barely perceptible—but not imaginary!—breath, as if he's bracing himself. Slides in. And the peck—the driest, most chaste of pecks! Could it be any clearer that he's grossed out, and hoping to avoid getting what I've got?

"I wonder how married couples keep from catching each other's stuff?" he asked aloud this morning.

An innocent-enough question, with an understandable motive. Who wants to get sick? But still it irked me. Nobody enjoys feeling like a pariah. It's lonely. And being shunned by your loving fiancé, in the middle of your supposedly blissful engagement, feels even worse. With a little effort, I can even blame him—and the wedding planning, with its related insane travel schedule and whirlwind of social obligations, *none of which I would be obligated to if it weren't for him*—for making me sick.

But whatever its true cause, my prenuptial cold is bringing one undeniable fact to light: Come what may, from here on out, when I need taking care of, this is the person who'll be doing the honors, just as I will be taking care of him, "in sickness and in health."

This pat phrase is among the first that come to mind when you think about marriage—in the abstract. But as we get closer to making that vow, promising to shoulder all of life's health burdens together feels like a very big deal.

On a minor level, we're learning that we have very different attitudes about almost everything related to health, nutrition, and fitness. I'm terrified of doctors and avoid them at all costs. I think the pharmaceutical industry can be evil. I'd prefer to cure everything with herbs and eagle feathers and a poultice of sheep's dung under a full moon.

Jonathan's motto is "Let's get it checked out!" He makes a good argument, too: If something's bothering me, wouldn't I rather know for sure what's going on, rather than sit around worrying? I tell him that phobias are irrational by definition, which usually ends the conversation.

Though I avoid Big Pharma, I don't assume the right to interfere in how he wants to be treated, especially since my beliefs are a bit outside the mainstream. It's his body, after all. But it's getting harder and harder to determine where he ends, and I begin. When we were just dating, it was a smaller matter, but now that we're in it for the long haul, how can I help feeling like I have a stake? He's delighted with a newfound one-pill-a-day fix for his chronic acid reflux; I am wary of the cumulative side effects of taking a synthetic drug every day of his life from here on out. How much better to modify the behavior; solve the problem at its root.

So do I argue my point of view? Try to convince him to modify his diet? I could, and I sort of have, but only to a point. Everyone has vices, of course, and so I fear the treacherous Bogs of Hypocrisy, and the Land of Tit-for-Tat, which appears to occupy a vast chunk of the territory of coupled life.

We did try making one pact. He drinks too much soda: bad for the body in general, and for his acid reflux in particular. I smoke on occasion: just plain bad. So we each pledged to limit ourselves to four a month. But it didn't feel good, monitoring each other like that, and there was a certain degree of retaliatory lighting up and Dr Pepper–guzzling, and, in the end, the agreement just sort of petered out.

We've had similar false starts with exercise. In general, I think it's fair to say that I value physical activity more than he does. While he golfed and shot a few hoops in high school, I ran cross-country and track. I've run marathons and adventure races; he's a champion napper. Of course, all that was before I moved to New York, got addicted to work, and then—the biggest crimp in my workout schedule—got engaged. (Which is especially funny to me because, according to popular lore, I'm supposed to be whipping myself into a workout frenzy right about now. I've even stoked the myth, having written for a certain popular wedding magazine about "bridal boot camps." Now that I'm in the thick of an engagement, I see that being a fiancée *is* a boot camp. Why on earth would you pay someone to torture you even more?)

But even if I'm not running much right now, and I'm lucky if I make it to yoga once a week, I *do* find time to ask Jonathan about his gym membership, to inquire politely whether he kind of maybe might think he should walk to work instead of taking the bus, and skip the elevator and take the stairs? I've caught myself arguing with him about what is and isn't "cardio." I've stopped short of my mom's tactic—buying the man in your life a pedometer for Valentine's Day, and asking for daily readouts—but just barely.

I'm not sure where this is coming from. I hope it's mostly love, and not projection. Maybe it's just wifely evolutionary hard-wiring, but I can't help but see him as a project of sorts, especially when it comes to food. He's a picky eater, and that frustrates me, because I hate to think of him missing out on all the incredible tastes in the world, all the stinky cheeses and slippery bivalves and exotic vegetables. And also because the plainer, even child-like foods he favors—the popcorn, the American cheese—have negligible nutritional value, while a widely varied diet is one of the simplest, most natural paths to good health.

But really—say it with me—I know that I can never change him. That only he can change himself. That I'm not his mother, and that, thank God, her work is already done, and done well. All I can do is hope that now he'll be a grown-up and take generally good care of himself, and beyond that, if something is a big enough deal to me—or, more accurately, threatening enough to our health as a couple—he will change. And that I'll do the same.

I'm reminded of a bizarre experience from college, back when I was in a sorority and we had gotten in trouble for something—drinking in the house, I think, because what else did we ever get in trouble for?—and the national organization flew out this representative to reprimand us. She was a nice white-haired lady in a nice suit and heels and she sat in a pink wing chair in our pink living room and told us a story about *responsibility*: She was a wife and had a home and a family to care for, and therefore she couldn't very well get drunk in the middle of the day and have her husband come home and see her that way, could she? We stared at her like she had poop on her shoe, shuffled out quietly, and mocked her later. It was a very out-of-touch lecture to give a group of nineteen- and twenty-year-old women in the late '90s, but now I see it in a slightly different light. *Damn, that lady wanted a martini.* And she held back because of someone else, and a promise she had made.

Right now, we're in the negotiation period: realizing what it is we'll be promising, determining exactly what we're in for. I know these boundaries will continue to slide as we get more and more entwined.

And at a certain point, it'll be moot. There will likely come a day when one of us makes all decisions for the other person.

Call me morbid, but I had the thought within a week of getting engaged: We're going to have to say good-bye someday. Joining my life with Jonathan's also means that I'll be there when our lives are severed, however it happens. To be completely honest, I've never thought more about death—my own, Jonathan's, our parents—than I do these days. It's as if a door has opened, and behind it there's a long hallway coming into view. I can't see the end, but now I know it's there.

> There will likely come a day when one of us makes all decisions for the other person.

> Inviting this wonderful thing into my
> life also means opening myself up to loss.

Part of it is probably just the out-of-body feeling you get when you complete any rite of passage. We're one step closer to "grown up," which means that, yup, we're aging. Our parents are aging. Our friends are aging. Having this wedding will be a wonderful way to mark time, but since we started planning it, life seems to be speeding up.

But it's more than that: Inviting this wonderful thing into my life also means opening myself up to loss.

Being a pretty resilient sort, I never saw love as much of a risk. But now that risk seems obvious, even if what I'm seeing right now is only a glimpse. It's enough of a glimpse that it's spurring my struggles to control his behavior, to keep him safe, to keep him around for as long as possible. We're entrusting parts of ourselves to each other, and it's a bizarre alchemy: The whole feels both stronger and more vulnerable than the sum of the parts.

Not long ago, I read Joan Didion's *The Year of Magical Thinking*. It's about her husband dropping dead of a heart attack while her daughter was in a coma. As she describes trying to believe that he's really gone, and reflects on their time together, Didion fills in the details of two lives that were thoroughly, remarkably meshed. They spent almost every single moment together. They shared a worldview, a collective brain. I was at once intensely envious of the depth and scope of their union—

an organism unto itself—and perversely aware of a silver lining should Jonathan and my differences ultimately keep us back from that perfect synchronicity: The end might not hurt as much.

> Being a pretty resilient sort, I never saw love as much of a risk. But now that risk seems obvious, even if what I'm seeing right now is only a glimpse.

But as much as some cowardly part of me might feel like that's an acceptable trade-off, I know that a halfway union is not what I want for Jonathan and myself. So I'm willing to engage, to duke it out over everything—and certainly over colds and carrots, pills and potions, doctors and the inevitable disease—to find a way to care for and honor each other. And when it comes to making our vows, we can't be afraid of naming the fears. The sickness, health, and, yes, until death do us part.

F WORDS OF WISDOM

Nagging never works. How many times do I have to tell you that? But seriously—worry as you might about someone else's health, you can only effect so much change. At this point in your relationship, it's especially crucial to realize that. You're marrying him, and all his bad habits; same is true in reverse. All we can hope is that life will take each of us to a place where we're motivated to kick them—for our own good, and that of the people who love us. And that our time together won't be cut short by anything that's within our direct control.

~

A "Modern Love" column in the *New York Times* by a woman named Amy Sutherland offers an interesting tip: While writing a book about animal trainers, she realized that the same techniques might prove effective with her husband. Now her mantra is "reward behavior I like, and ignore behavior I don't."

~

Many brides-to-be report more colds and other nagging health concerns than usual. Take good care of yourself during this process, and remember to take some time to be alone, though that's admittedly difficult when you have a job and life and a wedding to plan. One trick: sign up for an expensive weekly class—yoga, Pilates, spinning—that you have to pay for in advance. It provides structured exercise and "you" time every week, and you'll feel too guilty about the cost to skip.

~

As far as mental health is concerned, it's safe to say that a good share of the emotional craziness of the engagement period comes from a very deep, primal place. You're stepping out of the first half of life, and into the second. You're muddling the boundaries of your life with someone else's, and the more tangled together your roots become, the more it will hurt to separate them. You're promising to go all the way to the end of the line. That's a big deal. Though it comes out in small ways—wanting to be babied when you've got a cold, or blowing your top about a partner's bad habit— acknowledging the larger fear underneath can help you feel a lot better.

January 28

STUFF HAPPENS

The guilty pleasures—and future shock—of the wedding registry.

I'VE GOT a problem. It's not been officially diagnosed, but I'm pretty sure that this compulsion I feel to check our online wedding registry at least twice a day isn't healthy. I'm not sure I could stop if I wanted to, and there's no support group for women like me.

At first the concept of getting showered with gifts just because we're getting married felt uncomfortable. Presents? Attention? But we haven't really *done* anything to deserve it! It felt antiquated, too, a holdover from a time when first-time brides and grooms were young and needed help setting up house.

It's not that I'm anti-gift-getting. I like shredding wrapping paper as much as the next gal. I'm not anti-gift-giving, either. And I've gladly purchased gifts off dozens of registries, appreciating the guidance. But when it came to my own wedding, I was having a bizarre allergic reaction: It felt so public, so pushy, so excessive, and . . . so wrong. Shouldn't we just tell people to skip the gifts and make donations in our name?

At one point, I was dragging my heels so much that my future mother-in-law, Lynn, called to give me a little nudge, inquiring whether we would be registering, and where. I had more or less resigned myself to the notion by then—one more soul-crushing but necessary thing done by rote out of good manners, so the people whom you've invited to your wedding know what to do. And I was playing around with the I Do Foundation (www.idofoundation.org) to find most of our retailers, who would then donate a percentage of the price of each gift to a charity of our choosing. (I picked Girls Inc., because the Catholic Church, the church of my baptism and upbringing, had recently declared this network of after-school girls' clubs "pro-lesbian and pro-abortion." Priceless.)

But, as I told Lynn, Jonathan and I still hadn't chosen our china, crystal, or silver patterns. I'd been waiting for an extended trip home to Nebraska to go to Borsheim's, the Warren Buffet–owned mecca of all things sparkly, from gemstones to stemware. I planned on making two trips to the store, I heard myself explaining: one a sort of scouting mission, to follow up on some leads I had from trolling the Web, and to narrow down the choices to two or three in each area; and the second, with Jonathan, to make our final choices.

"Our."

As if there really were two people in this equation.

I imagine that a lot of women call most of the shots when it comes to choosing items for the registry, or at the very least take the lead. But we're on a different plane entirely: After all, I'm marrying the man who came home from a rummage sale at a magazine test-kitchen in his office building with a plastic beer pitcher and one of those little "thank-you" trays that they bring your check on at a diner.

"I remember when Marvin and I went to register," Lynn told me, referring to my future father-in-law, of course. "We walked in the door and within three minutes he had chosen everything, including pistol-handled silver and china with a cranberry-colored nautical motif. I didn't know what hit me. I had to go back later and change everything once I got my wits about me."

That made me laugh, both because I know how much Marvin still likes all things nautical, and because he has become a more judicious consumer over the years, and has offered us sound advice as we buy things for our wedding. But it also rang true, and sounded a sort of cautionary tale: Anyone can get overwhelmed in this bizarre process.

There are lots of different messages about what to buy— from advertisers, from family, from complete strangers, even— and there's pressure to make the right choice, to pick something with enduring appeal. "You'll have it for the rest of your life," someone says to me, oh, about once a day or so. But for the rest of what kind of life? What will that life look like, and how can I know now that the things I'm buying will match? City kitchen? Country kitchen? Big family? Small? Rich? Poor? And who'll be washing these dishes (floral? gilded? scalloped? plain?), and cooking in these pots? How will Jonathan and I share the roles of breadwinners and parents? It's hard enough to imagine where we'll be living and who we'll become over the next several decades, let alone pick patterns to fit.

But step outside the wedding whirlwind, which is kicking up all that pesky, obfuscating cultural dust, and, presto! they're not totems anymore. They're just plain old material possessions again, and chances are we won't *really* have most of them for the rest of our lives—not complete sets, anyway. A saucer will break here, a spoon get mangled by the garbage disposal there. They may be precious objects, but that's all they are.

Between that mantra, the guilt-assuaging aspects of the I Do Foundation, and, yes, a weakness for pretty things, I eventually got into the registry spirit. The actual process is entertaining. We didn't register in any physical stores, so we didn't have the "shoot-'em-up" pleasure that's most people's standard mental image of walking through a store, pointing that gun at everything you crave. But it was almost more fun to do it online. Sometimes when I shop online I put stuff in my cart and don't actually buy it, because the clicking itself is gratifying. Registering online feels the same way. Outside of a couple small com-

> It's hard enough to imagine where we'll be living and who we'll become over the next several decades, let alone pick patterns to fit.

plaints—I think it's horrifying to e-mail your whole registry list to people to announce that you've set it up, and I don't love it that you can see who bought what via your "thank-you list," thus ruining the surprise (or the one tattered remnant of surprise, anyway)—it works pretty well. It's like the shopping sprees I imagined when I was a kid.

I registered for every cookbook I've ever drooled over, for a Cuisinart, for some adorable kitchen towels. I clicked on some pretty Le Creuset pieces for color, and on some sturdy, humble cast iron pieces. I picked out a recycled glass bowl, scrap-wood measuring spoons, and towels made from unbleached organic cotton. I chose a "rebounder," a.k.a. a mini trampoline, just because Jonathan said we couldn't possibly fit one in our apartment. (It folds for easy storage—so there.) And, yes, I registered for a KitchenAid stand mixer, which, at the moment, seems to be material marital icon number two, after the engagement ring. I wasn't going to, but my co-worker Marnie was appalled. "When else are you going to have the chance to register for one?" she asked, incredulous that I hadn't put it on our list. "My sister and I have a pact that we're buying each other one for our thirtieth birthdays if we're not married by then."

The kid in me enjoyed herself very much. So did the ego-centric adolescent. Like so many things about a wedding, the items you choose for your registry tell people who you are— "Gee, don't I have great taste?"—and it feels good when someone gushes over something you've selected. The small sliver of adult in me, however, remains somewhat conflicted, despite the compulsive registry-checking behavior. It's a shopping spree, yes, but is the price tag my old identity? In my everyday life, as opposed to my "bridal life," I've been trying to shed possessions, not acquire them. I keep hearing my grandma repeating her favorite Depression-era slogan—*Use it up, wear it out, make it do, do without*—and I feel guilty for asking for all this stuff I don't really, truly need. At the same time, I'm being selfish, too, and skittish, not wanting to be burdened or weighed down. I'm still not totally sure I want all these trappings, these many things that will arrive in scores of boxes, boxing me into my new life as a married person.

Plus, I tend to value the old, from vintage clothes to flea market teacups, more than the new. When I moved into my first solo apartment after college, I took some of my parents' everyday stoneware with me. I still have it and use it and love looking at it, remembering it set against yellow straw place mats, one of them with a crystalline drop of amber syrup trapped between the fibers, fossil record of a Sunday morning Swedish pancake feast. Remembering those mornings while looking at those dishes makes me feel safe. I'm reluctant to replace them, loathe to give that up.

But, come to think of it, those dishes were on my parents' registry. Which means I'm not shopping only for me. I know Jonathan and I weren't thinking only of ourselves when we registered for Scrabble, my favorite board game, and Clue, his—and those are some of my favorite gift requests, because when I think about them they take me into the future, with visions of playing them in front of a fireplace somewhere, with each other, with friends, and, when I dare to think that far, with kids.

Even plates make me think of the future, as well as the past, principally when I think about their numbers. How many people will we have around our table at Thanksgiving, Christmas, Passover? Our lives are so full with wonderful family and friends now; I hope that bounty grows. Most people say eight settings will do, maybe ten if you really have a lot of space. Space is something we definitely do not have much of at the moment. But if the number of settings is a metaphor for abundance, I'm going to go all the way.

Just tonight, we got a package in the mail, containing something we *hadn't* registered for: two gorgeous hand-painted mugs, cobalt blue with yellow aspen leaves. They're so beautiful that I want to drink coffee out of them every day from here on out. There's not one version of our future life that I can't imagine them fitting into. They arrived unannounced from Jonathan's mom's best friend, with a note saying that she had known Lynn for fifty-eight years, and that she loves Jonathan, and now she loves me, too. No custom or obligation in sight, just a pure, generous outpouring of happiness and good wishes.

At midnight, after I had washed out the mugs and put them on the kitchen counter, I went online, of course, for just one more peek before bed. I saw that someone had bought us our first piece of china. It made me smile. And then, I started crying, for so many reasons: astonishment at the generosity of near-strangers, gratefulness for the family and friends I'm gaining, and apprehension about the options, mobility, and, ultimately, freedom I'm giving up. I'm about to become someone who has cabinet after cabinet full of good tableware to look after. And that's only the beginning.

As for that all-important dish pattern, after much deliberation, I wound up hedging my bets. We've registered for half pure-white bone china—elegant, versatile, restrained—and half a lush, extravagant green chinoiserie print, with flowers and birds and a shiny silver rim. Half useful, half fanciful; all mixable and match-able. Twelve place settings of everything, please.

F WORDS OF WISDOM

Yes, go ahead and put everything your little heart desires on your registry. Your guests will thank you for it. If you want to give back in the process, consider the I Do Foundation. (www.idofoundation.org)

~

Go for the good stuff—the china, the crystal, the sterling silver. Wouldn't you rather have an heirloom than one more appliance you'll wind up selling at a garage sale someday?

~

If you do register for some appliances, try to avoid the single-use variety: If it makes only one thing, like ice cream, waffles, or juice, you probably can wait and acquire it later. A high-quality toaster oven or food processor is more versatile. And it's not like you won't ever have a chance to buy kitchen-ware again, though it's easy to get caught up in the registry frenzy and believe that's the case.

~

Borsheim's (www.borsheims.com) is little known outside the state of Nebraska but it's an excellent place to register— amazing discounts. Choose what you want elsewhere (on the manufacturer's site, for example), because Borsheim's site can be difficult to navigate, and because it's ideal to see things in person before you commit to them for life. Then register with Borsheim's by phone and they'll display your registry for online ordering. They also can special-order most anything, so don't worry if they don't stock the patterns you want. And now that Warren Buffet has become America's second-biggest philanthropist, you can feel good about doing business with him, too!

~

Don't be afraid to register for things that have nothing to do with kitchen or bathroom: books the two of you will use forever, like an atlas or a dictionary; movies you'll watch again and again, like a boxed set of Hitchcock films; a tent you'll take on camping trips until your knees are so arthritic you can't climb in anymore. It's great to be able to request these items and imagine the two of you enjoying them together for years to come.

February 7

WELCOME TO IN-LAW COUNTRY

A vacation with future family members can teach you a lot—about where you're going, and where you've come from.

IT'S STANDARD, but solid, relationship advice: You never really know someone until you've traveled together. Jonathan and I have traveled plenty, and we still learn new things every time we go away. I imagine that most engaged couples in America have at least one getaway under their belts—even if it's only the proposal weekend. But how many take a full-fledged vacation with their future in-laws?

Last week, we spent several days with the Cohens at their time-share in Palm Springs. Jonathan's brother Brian and his girlfriend, Lauren, were there, too. It was just the thing to break up a cold and gloomy New York winter.

I knew nothing about Palm Springs until I met Jonathan, who's been going there since babyhood, first when his maternal grandparents, whom he calls Abba (Hebrew for "father") and Mom Rosie, had a home there, and later for the yearly Coachella Valley Music and Arts Festival. I attended the festival with him last spring and had a great time, though I didn't feel an enormous affinity for the place. We had just gotten engaged, and, at his parents' suggestion, went to check out the Westin hotel property (where they have the time-share) as a possible wedding venue. After about three minutes of walking around the manicured grounds, I was ready to run straight back to the car. Yes, the views of the mountains were stunning, the air was fresh, the flowerbeds artfully planted and dazzlingly bright. But the waterfall in the middle of the compound was fake, and so were the rocks the clear water tumbled over, and the whole man-made-oasis-in-the-middle-of-the-desert thing just wasn't working for me. Arriving for my wedding in a golf cart? Saying our vows in view of a swimming pool? No, thank you.

This Cohen family vacation was my second trip to the Westin, and I vowed to be more open minded. But still, somehow, even after several days' exposure to the rushing (fake) waterfall; the gentle, scented breeze; and the piped-in Andean flute music, I didn't really feel rejuvenated.

That puzzled me. It was a nearly effortless, easygoing trip. We quickly fell into a routine. The boys played golf, and the girls went to a leisurely breakfast, the flea market, the spa. Of course, we took care to meet up from time to time ("Come watch us putt on the ninth green!"), and always spent our evenings as a big group, but the days were more or less segregated. I wasn't sure why that made me uneasy. I don't golf. Nobody could love breakfast, flea markets, or spas more than I. Lynn and Lauren are delightful company. So why on earth was I dissatisfied? Am I really that ungrateful and uptight?

I've come to the conclusion that it wasn't so much *what* we were doing, but the mere fact that we were doing it separately that felt foreign, and therefore unnerving. In the Bare family, it's all for one and one for all, and too damn bad if you aren't interested in the Dada exhibit or the fourteenth shoe store of the day or Mark Twain's childhood home. Maybe you can get away with pacing impatiently up and down the sidewalk outside. But you can't go off and do anything else. It just isn't done. This isn't just when we travel; when my brother and I are home for visits, the same rules apply. We can make a group outing out of a car wash and a trip to the sporting-goods store. Go ahead— analyze away. But at this point it's simply how we do things, and it isn't going to change. So I suppose what I felt with the Cohens was a sort of low-level homesickness.

I also felt sort of guilty about being in that beautiful place without my mom and dad and brother, and that feeling cranked up my ever-present, low-level guilt about living so far away from my family a few notches. Add those two things together, and by the time I called home I was feeling like a kid at her first sleepover. I tried to be cheery, and brave. I found myself abbreviating stories, watching my word choice, trying not to sound too happy or not happy enough. I tried to ignore the notes of wistfulness, and maybe even envy, in my mom's voice. But there was no way around it: I felt bad. Bad for having fun without them, for being warm while they were cold, for being treated to the kind of lavish vacation that they rarely take. Bad for spending some of my precious leisure time with my "new" family. And, ultimately, bad for getting married, and leaving them behind. That's been one of the hardest things about being engaged: Beginning to see the size and shape of the hole I'm leaving in my first family, while trying to carve out a new place in my second family at the same time.

I haven't left yet, though. And I suppose I never will, altogether; maybe I'll just straddle the two territories until Jonathan and I have really jelled into a third family of our own, something solid of which both sets of in-laws can claim a piece. Because I still don't feel like one of the Cohen kids, accepting all this generosity like a birthright. Lauren and I went to the spa one morning and loaded up on treatments, charging them on our own credit cards. Later we were horrified to learn that Marvin had called up and insisted that they be rebilled to the room. He wouldn't take no for an answer. I'm used to letting my own dad pick up the tab, but Jonathan's? I'm not family, yet, but I'm being treated that way. It's wonderful, but overwhelming, and a little embarrassing.

Speaking of embarrassment, at several points during the trip

> That's one of the hardest things about being engaged: Beginning to see the size and shape of the hole I'm leaving in my first family, while trying to carve out a new place in my second family at the same time.

I had the odd feeling of checking myself, of holding back something that I ordinarily would have blurted out. I guess I still don't fully feel like myself around Jonathan's family. On one hand, it's good to realize that, because it gives me more empathy for the way he interacts with *my* family, which is noticeably different from how he is when the two of us are alone. I'm often goading him to "show more of his personality" when we're all together, so now I've had a taste of my own medicine.

But on the other hand, I know that I made my own trap. All those gorgeous mountains to climb, and me stuck in the valley, "relaxing" by the pool. I did have a few things on my wish list for this trip: long hikes, vintage-clothing shopping, drinking at mod bars in renovated '60s-era motels, finding where the gay men with fabulous taste hang out and doing as they do. Yet I wasn't quite comfortable speaking up and suggesting activities. It felt better to go with the flow.

I felt most like myself the evening we went for a hike in Indian Canyon, something suggested by one of the others, and eagerly seconded by me. Walking among ancient fan palms, hopping across streams, and scampering up steep hillsides like a mountain goat, I breathed more deeply than usual. I also found myself talking more, telling stories about Bare family trips to California and Colorado, our own experiences in nature.

There was another breakthrough, too. On the second-to-last morning of the trip, we all had breakfast with a woman named Liz, and her darling grandson David. Liz had been housekeeper and caretaker for Lynn's parents during much of their time in Palm Springs. Her real name is Luz, but Mom Rose renamed her Liz. That pretty much sums up the relationship. Yet Luz/ Liz truly cares for this family, and feels bonded to it. She was so excited to see Lynn, and her delight that the boys she used to scold and feed are all grown up was genuine.

I guess I just don't have any models for the singular relationship people have with domestic employees. Some of the stories they were telling—and laughing uproariously about—made me cringe. But there were sweet stories, too, and over the course of the meal I started to lose myself in their reverie. After that breakfast, I really started to get it: This was a nostalgia trip; they were all tapping into something that I couldn't quite feel or see. I'm sure that nostalgia always will be a powerful force on future visits to Palm Springs, and as we accumulate shared history, I'll feel more and more like I belong.

In the meantime, though, when we're together under circumstances like these, what's important to them is important to me. However they do things, that's how I'll try to do things, too. I won't completely bury my own desires, or my point of view, but I will do my best to get into the groove, or at least merge my groove with theirs. Likewise, I'll expect as much of Jonathan when we're spending time with the Bares. If we can stay flexible, and stay loose, we just might be able to temporarily bend ourselves to become what each family needs and expects, without materially changing our shape—as individuals, or as a couple. And in the right measure, our lives should be richer for it. After all, doing as the locals do is the only way to travel.

F WORDS OF WISDOM

There's nothing like taking a trip together for providing a crash course in the other family's way of doing things. If you can do that on each side during your engagement, you'll come out ahead on your wedding day, and beyond.

~

You really can't put a person in context until you've seen and interacted with them in the place, or places, they hold most dear, whether that's their hometown, a favorite vacation spot, or anyplace else. And spending time in a place that holds special memories for your partner, and beginning to feel at home there, can really bring you closer.

~

No matter the setting, when you're spending time with the in-laws, your mantra should be "go with the flow." You may well feel like a cat being petted the wrong way—but if you can temporarily suspend your wants and expectations, and tap into the way they do things, you may find that you're enjoying yourself, and seeing things from a new perspective. Of course, it's a delicate balance—no one should have to endure anything truly uncomfortable—but you'll know when you've reached that line. Begin by trying to see your new family through your partner's eyes, and see if that changes the way you approach them. The good news is that you have years ahead of you to decipher the new-family dynamics!

February 20

MAMA MIA!

Simply put, it wouldn't be a wedding without the family angst. But this may be the most complicated part of the whole process.

I'VE COME TO THE CONCLUSION that being the mother of the bride is no idyllic picnic-lunch reception. Much of this conclusion is based on the fact that being the *daughter* of the mother of the bride hasn't exactly been a rehearsal-dinner sunset pleasure cruise, either. (I'll sum up what we've fought about in one word: Everything.) But there are other clues that anyone can see, such as how hard it is for an M.O.B. (or an M.O.G, for that matter) to find something to wear.

If it's hard to find a flattering bridesmaid's dress, the search for an M.O.B. dress is even more loaded and difficult. Clothes in general are a sore spot for women my mother's age—they will be for me someday, too. Clothes for a day as important as your child's wedding are extra tricky. Beyond that, the stuff that's sold as "mother of the bride" wear is low quality and criminally ugly. And then the final insult: When you're shopping on the Web or flipping through a catalog, even the classier

If it's hard to find a flattering bridesmaid's dress, the search for an M.O.B. dress is even more loaded and difficult.

togs are displayed on bodies that I'd bet have never mothered a thing. "You are well within your rights to think I'm a bitch for saying this, but why do they show them on twenty-somethings?" my mom asked one day, completely exasperated. I told her that she had an excellent point.

She's got many excellent points, actually. From conversations with my mother, I've gathered that a typical M.O.B. deals with wedding stresses twice: once from her own perspective, and again from her daughter's. (The mother of the groom experiences much of the same stuff, minus having to work quite so closely with the bride, in most cases.)

A typical M.O.B. deals with wedding stresses twice: once from her own perspective, and again from her daughter's.

Many times, that perspective has eluded me, and I know that's one of the roots of our nastiest fights. But there are a few things I'm slowly beginning to understand: First, the engagement and wedding mark the end of an era for our parents, too. Our moms now have someone else to mother, if they so choose, but also other people with whom they must share their precious child, and, eventually, their grandchildren. That part is especially bittersweet when families are scattered across the country, like ours, because everybody knows they'll never get as much access as they want. Lynn, especially, has been up front about this, mentioning outright that she knows that the father's parents naturally tend to get shortchanged.

Second, for Jonathan and me, at least, there's an extra layer of angst on both sides of the family: Our parents are marrying us off right around the time that their own surviving parents need them more than ever. It's a collision that's no doubt leaving them crunched, both time-wise, and emotionally. I've heard them called the "sandwich generation," and that rings especially true right now, when my grandparents and Jonathan's require more and more care just as wedding demands are heating up.

Then there's the event planning: My mother is just as invested as Jonathan and I in making sure that the wedding is gorgeous, and that all guests feel welcome and cared for. Maybe even be more invested than we are. The same goes for Lynn, who's getting into the action in her own way. Their friends are coming, too, and the success or failure of the event will reflect on them, perhaps even more acutely than it will on us. I've realized that in parent circles, wedding stuff makes up a big swatch of the social fabric—I think my mom spends more time going to showers and weddings than I do.

Finally, I can't underestimate the impact of the fact that marrying off a child is new territory for both our moms—Jonathan and I are both the eldest children in our families. I bet by the time my brother gets hitched my mom will have loosened up considerably—just as she did with his curfew.

But family weddings are not entirely foreign ground, of course, and therein lies a complicating factor: I've found that the shadow of my mom's own wedding has loomed large in the planning of mine. As in so many other areas of my life, she wants me to be like her, but not; to emulate the things she loved and valued about her own wedding, but avoid the things she'd prefer to forget. It's the classic mother-daughter scenario: They see our weddings, and even our marriages, as do-overs for their own. Since I got engaged, she's told me things that I honestly would prefer not to know. But I understand that I need to hear what she has to say, because that's part of growing up, both in terms of gaining a more three-dimensional understanding of your parents' lives, and becoming the keepers of their legacies.

My dad has been less forthcoming with his feelings about the fact that I'm getting married, and with his opinions about how I'm choosing to do it. No surprise there—he's a classic dad in that regard, the "if you're happy, I'm happy," glad-to-have-the-Y-chromosome-excuse guy who'll just be in the other room watching football. I don't want to invade his privacy, so I haven't tried to draw him out, but I do hope that we can find a way to communicate about the wedding someday, maybe when the action has subsided a little. It makes me sad to think of him as all checkbook and no voice.

That's not my only regret where my parents, or Jonathan's, are concerned. It's probably too late in this process to do more than apologize for not taking more of their wants and needs into consideration, and for being too busy dealing with my own issues (see also the other twenty-two chapters of this book) to take the time to decipher the emotions woven into their half of the terse phone conversations, planted behind the tight smiles.

I am proud of one thing, though. This weekend, I left aside mounds of work and wedding planning, and took the bus down to Washington, D.C., alone, without Jonathan. I gave up my time completely to my parents, who were in town visiting my brother. It was just the four of us again, and we spent our time visiting galleries in Georgetown, traipsing around the Mall, and taking the metro to its outer limits for the real purpose of the trip, at least for me: a barnstorming, take-no-prisoners mother-of-the-bride-outfit mission.

Yes, my dad and Brad came, too. The two of them were skulking around the men's department when we found it. I walked out of the dressing room and called my dad on his cell, telling him to come up the escalator and take a look. It was a light green St. John's Knits suit, with buttons made from dark, pearly shell; it was a perfect color for her, and it fit perfectly, too. She looked beautiful. And she was smiling—a real smile, full of happiness, and also relief. I recognized the look, because I've seen it in the mirror a few times lately. In this alien process, she'd stumbled upon something that felt comfortable, something that felt like *her*.

We bought it without hesitation.

Helping find it was the least I could do.

F WORDS OF WISDOM

People take Tolstoy too literally: Every happy *and* unhappy family is different from one another. There's no right or wrong way for you and any of the parents who might be in your wedding orbit to interact. But it's extremely difficult to find a bride who hasn't fought with one or both of her own parents during the process of planning a wedding—and in-law skirmishes are more common than not. Don't despair.

~

Parents often try to play out their own wishes (and frustrated ambitions) on the stage of their children's lives, and that goes triple for weddings. This may not be news to you, but sometimes even the most basic truths can slip out of perspective in the heat of wedding planning. Where mothers are concerned, remember that in some cases a daughter's wedding is their first real opportunity to be in control, since their own mothers ran away with theirs.

~

Be aware that, in general, parents are extra-sensitive during this time of your life. They are quite likely sad about "losing" you to this marriage, and to a new family, whether they express that to you—or are even conscious of the fact—or not. Be generous with your time, and no matter how crazy they are driving you, be as gentle as you can possibly stand to be. When you scream at them, as you inevitably will, apologize.

~

Dress your mother in St. John—or any other designer attire she desires. She's worth it.

March 3

LET'S HEAR IT FOR THE GIRLS

Finding bridesmaids' dresses will never be easy. But it's about so much more than that.

I'VE JUST SPENT an afternoon shopping with some of my bridesmaids, trying to help them find something to wear to the wedding. At one girly little boutique in the West Village, the salesclerk asked when I was getting married.

"May twentieth," I told her.

"Oh good—you're legit," she replied. "Some people come in here so far in advance that we don't even have the right season's merchandise in yet!"

I took that as a little pat on the back. I've tried to be nontraditional and laissez-faire about the wedding-party thing. Their outfits aren't going to match—we've requested that the women wear dresses of any style, in the pink/peach/coral color family, and that the men wear dark suits and pink(ish) ties. Their numbers don't match, either: I have seven bridesmaids; Jonathan has three groomsmen. We also have two "best men," our two brothers. (I wanted to have them "ordained" on the Internet, so they could jointly perform the ceremony, but that idea was a bit too out there for my parents.)

I think I lapped up the salesclerk's praise because I'm feeling anxious that my attempts to relax this process have actually made things harder—for the people in our wedding party, and also for me. I find myself spending a lot of time worrying about whether my bridesmaids feel put upon or stretched, and trying to avoid making them do any silly things they don't want to do. I didn't even want to call them brides*maids*. Whether you read the second half of the word as "maiden" or "servant," I don't love the connotation. But what else to call them? Believe me, I thought and thought and came up with nothing but ridiculous options. "Stand-up gals"? Brideswomen? Ugh.

> I'm feeling anxious that my attempts to relax this process have actually made things harder—for the people in our wedding party, and also for me.

I'm starting to see why people fall back on the traditional where dresses are concerned, too. Maybe it's agony for a conscientious bride to find one dress that every bridesmaid can wear relatively comfortably, but once it's been selected, you're more or less shielded from any grumbling: It's part of the Bridesmaids' Code never to complain (to the bride, at least) about the getup. Like any uniform, everyone just wears it, case closed.

Not that my bridesmaids are whiny or difficult—quite the opposite. But the "wear whatever you want" decree I made several months ago may not be quite the bright idea I thought it was. Here's my logic: Giving them a color family, rather than a single hue, would not only look interesting, but also be more considerate, because each of them could pick a flattering color. Same goes for style. I want everyone in our wedding to feel confident that they look good, and have the kind of fun you can have only when you're not tugging on an ill-fitting dress all night. And, after all, they manage to dress themselves quite stylishly every day, so I felt completely confident giving them free reign.

Plus, I figured that at least some of them would already own something suitable. At the moment, it appears that three of seven do. Meredith is wearing her grad school graduation dress. Mary resurrected something she bought when she and I were shopping in New Orleans years ago, visiting Joyce, another bridesmaid, who was living there at the time. I think that Joanne—who has more clothes and better taste than 99.9 percent of the female population—just opened her closet, closed her eyes, threw a dart, and hit the perfect thing. She may even wind up providing loaners for some of the other girls.

Success stories—yee-haw! Saving money! Saving time! Making things easy! Witness the Low-Key Wedding operating like a well-oiled machine. However . . . not everybody has a pink/peach/coral summer dress in her closet, and there's where the potential for anguish creeps in.

Sara, a Bluefly.com addict, didn't have much trouble. She loves to shop online, and because she's a rail-thin endurance athlete, everything looks good on her. It's not much of a risk for her to buy something without trying it on. And Bluefly is the perfect Web site for a task like this one, since you can refine categories by size and color and come up with a targeted selection from their vast inventory.

But those of us who need to worry a bit more about draping and gaping and bulging and the like are relegated to shopping in the physical world. Hence today's excursion. We managed to pick about the coldest, most blustery March day on record to go shopping. At lunch beforehand, I was already cranky, nervous about being the center of attention. Even though we were only a party of four (Joyce couldn't make it), it was still my party. Joanne, who was there to provide moral support and black-belt shopping skills, pointed out that the time of year was getting everyone down. So we, and our March blahs, sallied forth.

We hit a couple department stores, and then boutiques, boutiques, boutiques, and found many things that were almost really great, but . . . not . . . quite. In midafternoon, my attention wandered. I was more interested in combing the racks for something to wear to my upcoming shower, or sinking into a chair and staring into space, than participating in the relentless quest for pink, pink, pink. One thing that hadn't occurred to me is that we'd be at the mercy of the season's color trends; it seems to be a black, white, lavender (ick), and green kind of year. It got to the point where we could stand in the middle of a store, do a quick 360-degree scan, and make a beeline to the right section— or, more frequently, just turn around and leave.

When one of the girls would find a potential winner, and put it on, I'd form an opinion about how the dress looked, of course, but I'd also look into her eyes, trying to discern how she was really feeling. Beautiful? Ridiculous? Sexy? Fat? I'd also glance at the price tag, hoping it was within budget. It's just not easy to find an affordable dress that makes you feel fabulous; I know that as well as anybody. And as they dressed and undressed, and dressed again, I started to realize that while I had wanted these women to buy something for themselves, no matter how I try to rationalize it, they're really buying something for *me*.

So is it lazy—even wrong—to deflect the potentially tedious search for that very specific something onto them?

I know it's too late for that question, so I'd better just give in to it. They're doing this because I've asked them to, and I've asked them to because people ask their friends to do such things, and nobody gets that ticked off about it. Period. And that's sort of the conclusion I've come to about having a wedding party, in general.

Jonathan and I actually considered not having attendants at all, for the sake of simplicity and modernity. But thinking about

> I started to realize that while I had wanted these women to buy something for themselves, no matter how I try to rationalize it, they're really buying something for *me*.

getting married without our closest friends standing up there with us made me really sad, and Jonathan felt the same way. These are some of the most important people in our lives. They've helped us get where we are today, individually and as a couple. And the choices were obvious—we didn't agonize over whom to ask, which I take as another sign that we did the right thing. It just felt natural.

I'm honored and thrilled that they're willing to play this role, because I want to honor *them*, because I want them near me on one of the most monumental days of my life, and most of all because I love having an excuse to spend extra time with them in the run-up. Time is the most precious commodity in my life at the moment, and theirs, too, because they're all very busy people. Anything that makes us stop and be together, even if it's a highly ritualized affair, has got to be good. I felt the same way the two times I was asked to serve as a bridesmaid, both for people who are now returning the favor.

It is kind of sad that it takes a big event like this, and all this money, and all this trouble, to cause me to spend more time with people I love. It's one of the things that makes me worry about the way we live our lives today. I am glad, though, that there seems to be a trend toward finding a way to do something important and splashy with your best friends even if you aren't getting married. In particular, I've noticed that people are having big thirtieth-birthday blowouts. Two male friends had a softball game, with homemade T-shirts for each team and a big barbecue afterward. Meredith's boyfriend threw her a fake prom, complete with decorations, a photographer to snap pictures with your date, programs, a "prom committee," and, of course, a prom court. (Naturally, she got to be queen.) Other people have had big bowling parties, or massive open-bar nights. A friend of a friend even had a huge *Dirty Dancing: Havana Nights*–themed weekend event in Miami, complete with a Web site detailing the event, and a registry.

And why not? I think that some of the panic people—OK, women—feel about getting married before a certain age could be relieved, or at least channeled in a productive direction, if there was a culturally mandated rite of passage for *individuals* on the occasion of their thirthieth birthdays, to celebrate who they've become and what they've accomplished to date. (The thirtieth birthday as the new bar mitzvah/*quinceanera,* anybody?)

The fact that Jonathan and I are both about to turn thirty may be influencing how we're planning this wedding more than we realize. I'd be lying if I said we didn't take those milestones into consideration when setting our wedding date—I've mentioned it before. And if we were much older, I think it would be a smaller affair, for sure. As is, it's shaping up to be one big hurrah to celebrate several important moments in our lives.

When I view it that way, I'm extra-thrilled that I've got this big crew of extraordinary people by my side. Though I definitely am relating to each them in different ways. Or, rather, to the different camps—marrieds and the singles—in different ways.

I find that I talk to the three married bridesmaids much more about the process, about how I'm feeling. I try out more questions and scenarios on them—ranunculus vs. roses, buffet vs. sit-down dinner, protocol issues involving all the various players in the big day. It makes perfect sense, of course, because they've been through this before. But I'm also aware of not wanting to bore the singles to tears, and, more than that, not wanting to . . . well, *throw in their faces the fact that I'm getting married, and they're not.*

There, I said it. It's such a sticky thing to write about. I feel weird even thinking about it. Because it's not like my four single bridesmaids are dying to get hitched, as far as I know. It appears that they feel much the way I did before Jonathan proposed: Marriage is dandy, if it comes up at the right time and with the right person, but it's not a big fat brass ring to be snatching at whenever a potentially desirable situation might come into view, and it's certainly not mandatory. Their lives are far too rich for them to be thinking that way.

But there's this cultural vibe we're all subject to, this idea that getting married is still a prerequisite for a female life well lived. If you wind up getting divorced, fine. *But for God's sake, get married once, lest other people think there's something wrong with you!* It's such an ugly, antiquated, antifeminist thing to articulate—but you have to admit that it's still in the ether, no matter how hard we try to exorcise it. And I suppose that's what I'm tapping into, and dancing around: The idea that getting married is something that all women want, sooner or later, whether they discuss it with you or not, and that the older you get, the more you want it. *So when you're the one getting married, be polite and don't dangle anything in front of anyone else's nose, OK?*

I'd been warned—and read in various places—that things could get strained with single friends during my engagement. *Strained* is not the word that I would use. You can't make a Bridget Jones caricature out of these women. But there has been a feeling in the air, a tinge of wistfulness, maybe, and one day something bubbled to the surface.

I was leaving Joanne's apartment after a day spent working on place cards and program design. We were talking and laughing as she walked me to the elevator and pushed the button for me, because I was weighed down with multiple bags and an enormous wrapped wedding gift she had just handed me.

"I wish you weren't getting married," she blurted.

The sentiment didn't surprise me, because I had sensed it, and I've felt variations of it myself in the past, but I was shocked—and impressed—that she had said it out loud.

"Oh, Jo. Did you feel this way about your other married friends?" I asked.

"No, but you're more fun. I'm worried that we won't have as much fun together anymore," she said, smiling sadly.

I was glad for her honesty, and admired her for it. But I really wasn't sure what to say. Because it does happen, doesn't it? People get married, and they disappear. I've started to fade away already, like Michael J. Fox's family photo in *Back to the Future*. Being engaged just does it to you; all the demands on your time, all the new people in your life. I gave her the best promise I

> People get married, and they disappear.
> I've started to fade away already, like
> Michael J. Fox's family photo in *Back to
> the Future*. Being engaged just does it to
> you; all the demands on your time, all
> the new people in your life.

could, without dismissing her concerns. I told her I would do my best to stay fun, to make time.

If I don't, I'm counting on her to call me on it. In the meantime, I'm thrilled with my bridesmaids, all seven of them. And I'll be mindful of planning outings with them that have absolutely nothing to do with the wedding, too. And, come to think of it, maybe I made the right dress decision after all. Maybe I'm glad that I've sent them on this wild goose chase for the perfect pink dress—if it means that we'll have to go shopping together again next weekend, and the weekend after that.

F WORDS OF WISDOM

People are so bought into this cultural notion of brides behaving like Imelda Marcos on acid that you may find your girlfriends—married and single—are impressed with any crumb of non-wedding-related attention you throw them. It's nice of them to cut you so much slack, but you know you're bigger than the stereotype. All the rules of friendship that applied before you got engaged are still in full effect.

~

Your bridesmaids are doing you an enormous favor. It's expensive and time consuming and also can be emotionally trying. Be grateful. And remember to ask about their lives, and to try to do the same kinds of things together that you did before you got engaged. With less free time, it's hard, but you can make it happen. Try having people over for brunch or drinks, an efficient way to see lots of friends in one fell swoop, bridesmaids or not. It feels good to be able to give a little something back to people who are doing so much for you.

~

It's easy to get into tiffs with friends you *didn't* choose to be in your bridal party, mainly because that can be awkward. But avoiding the person because of the awkwardness is a fatal mistake. Every friendship has different operating instructions and quirks, but in general, if someone is upset, and they've let you know as much, or you can just tell, it's like any other slight, real or perceived: The hurt will likely heal with time. But the more you can do to pay attention to and take care of that person in the interim, even if they ignore you for a while, the better you'll both come out of it at the end.

~

Err on the side of extreme caution in how frequently you talk about your wedding with single friends. If you pay attention, you can often sense negative vibes, ranging from mild annoyance to full-on loathing, coming off brides' single friends. (Anyone's, not just yours.) When that single person is one of your bridesmaids, it's even more crucial. Almost everyone knows someone with a friendship that "just faded away" (or maybe even ended with a bang) after a bridesmaid gig, right? Think about it—was the bridesmaid single? Not to say that your single bridesmaids automatically won't want to talk wedding with you, but that it's probably best to let them take the lead. In the course of conversation, let your single friends bring up the wedding, rather than you saying something first. (The exception, of course, being tactical bridesmaid-related stuff, which you can probably cover in the occasional brisk—but not bossy—group e-mail.)

~

Lean more heavily on your married friends for wedding-related advice. They've been there, and they can take it.

March 14

MISSING MANNERS

In which The Bride attends three showers, lays down the etiquette law, and makes a few bloopers of her own.

I WAS INVITED to a wedding shower a while back. The invitation was lovely—an intricately decorated, teapot-shaped card, heralding an afternoon tea party in honor of the bride, a friend of Jonathan's. We were going to the wedding, and though it was tricky to carve out time to attend the shower, I appreciated the invitation, and looked forward to getting a little more familiar with the bride and her friends before the event.

Anxious to make a good impression, I spent quite a bit of time choosing just the right gift, searching for something thoughtful, appropriate, and fun—but not too racy, seeing as I barely know the bride. I settled on a Tibetan-inspired cotton tunic, from a little shop that I love, to wear on her beach honeymoon. I even dragged Jonathan along and—to his dismay—consulted him about which color she would like best.

Then I got an e-mail.

The tea party would be held at a local tea shop, said the e-mail, and the price would be twenty-five dollars per person,

payable to the shower hostess. (Who, I later learned, is independently wealthy. But that's neither here nor there.)

I . . . was . . . APPALLED. Truly. Outraged. I didn't shut up about it for days. Where I come from, the hostess pays. Period.

But my outrage didn't stop me from going, and I had a good time. The bride was sweet and gracious; the hostess was charming, with a cool job and lots of interesting stories to tell. The gift seemed to be well received, and so (though I swear I would disown any child of mine for what those women did) all was more or less forgiven.

Until a thank-you note failed to arrive. And, to date—weeks and weeks and counting—still no note.

I know that my boundless love of thank-you notes—sending and receiving—probably borders on OCD, but I can't help it. It's how I was brung up.

My righteous umbrage at this particular solecism is a colorful, cautionary backdrop for what I'm going through at the moment: perpetually swearing on *Tiffany's Table Manners for Teenagers* not to offend in a similar manner. In particular, my showers, the second of which is just past, required careful attention. Though must-dos and no-nos are scattered along the path to the altar like land mines, wedding showers seem to be particularly dangerous areas. I had two, which were also my first experiences with being the bull's-eye center of attention, dress rehearsals for being The Bride. My shower in Akron was first, an elegant country-club luncheon with an "around-the-clock" theme thrown by a group of Jonathan's mom's friends. They went out of their way to make me feel special. Hors d'oeuvres were passed, gorgeous flowers arranged, cookies at every plate decorated with the *exact number of hours* until our wedding ceremony. My bridal privileges included the best seat in the house, tulle on my chair, and a beautiful white corsage.

> Though must-dos and no-nos are scattered along the path to the altar like land mines, wedding showers seem to be particularly dangerous areas.

The gaggle of Girl Scouts having a fancy tea party in the lobby only added to the pinch-me-we-must-be-playing-dress-up quality of it all: They were rehearsing what I was living. As I clicked past them in my high heels on the way to the club's lavish powder room, I felt as if I were walking back in time, as if they were the group I really belonged to. "Look! There goes a *bride*!" came the stage whisper as I passed. Thank goodness *they* knew who was who.

But if I was finally assuming a role I had practiced, and played at, for years, why—God, WHY?—when the first course was served, did I grab my dessert spoon and plunge it into the tomato bisque?

Mortifying. Such a simple thing, and so many people watching, and I screwed it up. I immediately recognized my mistake, switched utensils, and began fuming at myself. I know how to set a table! I know which fork to use! Don't I?

I had been similarly undone by shopping for a shower outfit. I had this innate sense of what it *needed* to be: conservative, feminine, pastel-y. But I also knew what I wanted: something sweet but not saccharine, city-chic but suburb-appropriate, kid-tested but mother-approved.

On that first shopping trip with some of my bridesmaids, I kept seeing clothes that made me think, "That's what someone would wear to a shower." But I just couldn't be that person, or buy those outfits. None looked like me. I've never looked for something that felt more like a hard-to-find costume for a very specific—and daunting—role.

I had barely bothered to shop for my wedding dress, deciding almost immediately to have it made, and found myself wishing that I could have had a shower outfit custom made as well. I eventually bought something at the last minute at a boutique in my neighborhood, a high-waisted, V-neck dress with cap sleeves that mixed girly styling with unconventional, hippie-ish fabric. I was happy with it, but I'm pretty sure my mother, who had flown in for the festivities, wasn't.

Speaking of the dress, while I sat there opening present after present, I found myself sweating—and yes, in that *never-let-them-see-you-sweat* kind of way. It was mortifying, and decidedly unbridal, pitting out my dress like that.

My gaffes at the first shower—grabbing the wrong spoon, the unseemly perspiration—were out of character. I can identify a soup spoon. I've never sweated profusely in public before in my life. Why those cracks in the facade, at that particular moment? Were they small, unconscious ways of fighting convention? My being uncomfortable in my new role? Signs that I was truly overwhelmed? Maybe I was just out of practice. I'd felt more socially adept at my seventh grade cotillion.

I saw *Roman Holiday* for about the twelfth time on a plane not long ago, and, boy, did I identify with Audrey Hepburn's Princess Ann. At that first shower, I had more grown women grabbing me by the hands and sizing me up than I knew what to do with. They were dear. I'm sure that they really were happy to meet me. But I also sort of felt like a piece of bridal meat.

My second shower, in Lincoln, felt more comfortable, because it was smaller, more casual, full of people I knew better . . . and didn't take itself as seriously. My dear, clever friend Stacy made the invitation, a funny homage to Julia Child, and everyone brought no-fail recipes and gifts of kitchen gear. It didn't hurt at all that the guests were my aunts and grandma, my best friends from childhood, and my Mom's best friends from childhood. It also didn't hurt that we were drinking Bloody Marys.

But in both cases, in different ways, I felt very honored, as well as tested. (More on that later, regarding bachelorette parties.)

I sort of felt like a piece of bridal meat.

It was good practice for the wedding, I suppose. I'm getting a clearer and clearer picture of what being a bride means, and it's not what I expected. I predict that I'll feel like a weird combination of hostess and guest of honor. As the wedding's raison d'être, I'll have certain social obligations, made more complicated by the fact that Jonathan and I each will have lots of guests we don't know very well. In planning the event, I've tended to think more about my peers than I do about extended family and family friends, probably because I'm so immersed in my peer group. I live in the city. None of my friends have kids; I don't spend any time with the elderly. But the wedding will include people of all ages, from all places and parts of our lives, and we'll need to know how to connect with them all.

Interestingly, some of the most memorable moments at both showers involved guests I don't know intimately, who were quite advanced in age. Jonathan's maternal grandpa, aka Abba, was the lone man at the Akron shower. "What's my role?" he'd asked earlier that day. "Just be one of the girls," replied his daughter, Jonathan's Aunt Susan.

He walked in looking dapper, slowed a bit by Parkinson's but sharp as ever, and even before he was introduced to my mom, he started crying. It took everything I had to hold it together, both because he is so sweet and because I didn't want to think about my mom thinking about her dad, who died before my fourth birthday. Bridesmaid Joanne, who, in an unbelievably generous gesture, had flown in to be by my side, started crying when she saw him cry.

In Nebraska, my mom's friend Cindy's mother, RuRu, gave

me the best gift. In keeping with the Julia Child theme, she gave me copies of *Bon Appétit* from the '70s with articles featuring Child, accompanied by a set of patio glasses, iced tea spoons, straws . . . and an admonition to make a good old American root beer float already.

My other favorite shower present was from someone of that generation, too. I'd never met Libby Rosenblatt before the Akron shower, but she gave me a fifty-dollar gift cerificate from Borders, and a card with a sentiment that put it over the top—that I should take some time for myself and read some books I enjoy. "I just had a feeling you were a reader," she said to me when she said good-bye, squeezing my hand, and, once again, I wanted to cry. In my happy-but-completely-overwhelmed state, a gift intended for "alone time," a break from all this wedding hoopla— and, most of all, something that had nothing whatsoever to do with being a wife—was the best gift of all.

By the end of that first marathon present-opening session, after more than an hour of exclaiming and smiling and trying to make grateful, enthusiastic eye contact with the right people when I opened their gift, I'm sure I looked anything but sincere. And I know I called a few people I'd just met by the wrong names. Even when you know the people you're interacting with very well, this stuff is exhausting. And when you're tired, well, you make mistakes.

But let's be honest: Even when I'm not tired, I make mistakes. Though I know that you don't *really* have a whole year after a wedding to give a gift, I routinely push it, especially when it comes to close friends. (A gift certificate for a nice dinner on their first anniversary usually smoothes everything over.) And I did have two showers, which many sources say is a no-no. So maybe I'm the tacky one, after all!

You never really, definitively know when you've violated the rules of etiquette, do you? That's the bitch: Etiquette demands that one gracefully turn the other cheek when its rules have been broken, so the response to a faux pas is silence. The Tea-Party Terrorists probably sleep peacefully at night. (Unless, of course, they've read this book. The Emily Post Institute condones the occasional public shaming, right? They do publish advice columns, after all.)

It's all rather passive-aggressive. Take, for example, the question of money as wedding gift. Can you ask for it? Well, *no*, most sources say—unless of course someone asks *you* what you would like. Then it's OK to say, "Actually, Aunt Fran, we're all about the Benjamins"? Which seems a little arbitrary, even to me, from all the way up here on my well-mannered high horse. But I won't hand down a decision on that one. No time, you see. Too busy writing thank-you notes.

F WORDS OF WISDOM

Not many of us get to experience being a princess, so being the guest of honor at a shower (and, of course, being a bride) may be as close as we'll ever come. Of course you're spoiled and pampered, but there's a flip side that's easy to forget: You must be gracious to, and interested in, absolutely everyone, and that can wear you out. Prepare yourself for how exhausting showers can be. Make sure you're rested and wearing something that makes you feel beautiful and comfortable. And no, it's not the time to wear your all-natural herbal deodorant. Go for the industrial-strength antiperspirant.

~

It's an incredible luxury to have at least one wingperson at any shower given by people you don't know very well. Anyone who is willing to do this for you, especially on top of other responsibilities related to your wedding, is worth their weight in gold.

~

Thank-you notes are always mandatory, but they're especially meaningful because so many wedding presents arrive by mail these days. Spare your guests the anxiety of wondering whether the postal service did its duty.

~

No matter how organized and careful you are, it's pretty much inevitable that you will forget to thank someone for something at some point during this process. When you screw up, smile, apologize profusely, and move on.

March 30

GOY MEETS BOY

When a Christmas-worshipping agnostic has her most powerful spiritual experience ever in a temple on Yom Kippur, it's safe to say that the kids will be raised . . . how exactly?

W E'RE NOT GOING to Akron for Passover this year. I can't help but automatically parse that sentence—the "Passover," the "this year," and most of all the "we're"—and laugh. "We" have celebrated only one Passover together so far, and I have participated in two total in my life, the first of them an informal grad school affair that involved a lot of (nonkosher) wine and zero Scripture.

If graphed, my exposure to Judaism over the years would show a steady upward trend. I grew up near one of the three synagogues in my hometown (population 275,000), but I didn't have a single Jewish friend or classmate until late junior high, and then only one or two. Then I attended a college with a large Jewish population, and joined a sorority which probably had more than 50 percent Jewish members—though I wasn't always sure who was what. (I once gave my blond, hazel-eyed pledge daughter, Dory Michaelson, an Easter basket.)

Sophomore year, I dated a Jewish guy two years older than me. When his family came to town for his graduation, I liked them immediately. I noticed that his father held his hand at dinner—on top of the table. That was different. And good.

The more I knew about Jewish people and their culture, the more at home I felt, and slowly, and in my own special shiksa way, I started to get it. Like most people from Christian backgrounds, I originally assumed that Hanukkah was a big-deal holiday—it's during the Christmas season, after all. Then I was invited to the aforementioned grad school Seder, and became a Passover fan. Finally, last year, I broke through. I knew what Yom Kippur was about in the abstract, but this was the first time I'd gone to a service. I was floored. I thought of all those born-again Christians of my high school days going on and on about a personal relationship with Jesus as the single means to salvation. There I was, so clearly not a member of the Tribe, more or less wandering into a synagogue and sitting down, and immediately I had tapped a vein, letting my sins and sorrows flow out and mingle with the sadness of the universe. I sat there and cried and cried while Jonathan squeezed my hand. It's my single most powerful spiritual experience to date.

Now I understand that autumn is the most important time of the Jewish year. And so I understand why what happened when we went to Akron to spend this past Thanksgiving with Jonathan's parents happened when it did.

It was Wednesday night, and we had done some cooking. Lynn was tidying up, and I was keeping her company, sitting at the kitchen table sipping blueberry tea, chatting, and alternately leafing through her first edition of Helen Gurley Brown's *The Single Girl's Cookbook* and happily applying stickers and stamps to our save-the-dates.

Marvin walked into the room. "Family meeting," he said, motioning toward the den. I started to get up, but then Jonathan gestured for me to stay. Confused, I sat back down. No one said a word; they just turned around and walked out. So I went back to my stickering and stamping, humming to myself. Maybe they were planning a surprise?

After they had been gone for fifteen minutes, I started to get curious. But the door was firmly shut; no sound escaped from underneath. At half an hour, my mind started churning with possibilities. At forty-five minutes, I was pretty sure that I had committed some kind of unspeakable faux pas, for which I was being shunned. At an hour, I was wondering if I should call the police. Multiple scenarios ran through my mind. Was there a gas leak? A murderous intruder? Had Jonathan—and his parents—decided that this upcoming marriage was a grave mistake, and snuck out the window and run away?

Around the hour-and-fifteen-minute mark, they trooped out, smiling but subdued. Jonathan's parents said good night and went up to bed. I looked at him quizzically, to say the least. He was wearing the "I'll tell you later" face.

Within the half hour, I had made him spill it.

Turns out that Marvin was too polite to say it in front of me, but he's worried about our religious future. Or, rather, our kids' religious future. He's concerned about us raising kids in a household where Mommy and Daddy don't believe the same things,

> If marriage is a binding contract, it makes sense to determine the terms beforehand, and while we don't have a lot of money to quibble over, it's not so far-fetched to think that there are emotional and cultural items worth negotiating.

or maybe don't believe anything at all. He believes that children need a religious foundation, and that they are too fragile to be forced to choose between two options, so the choice must be made for them. The preferred choice was unspoken, at least in the version of the story that Jonathan told me. But it was lurking so near the surface that I couldn't help but see it. Even though they'd have to convert, due to the laws of matrilineal descent, Marvin thinks our children should be raised Jewish.

He brought it up again this spring, in slightly different terms. What he wants, he said, is merely for the two of us to sort it out. To decide what we believe. To know in advance what the religious climate of our home will be like, so as to provide a consistent, solid backdrop for our family life.

I see his point. So does Jonathan. We understand the "prenup" idea. If marriage is a binding contract, it makes sense to determine the terms beforehand, and while we don't have a lot of money to quibble over, it's not so far-fetched to think that there are emotional and cultural items worth negotiating.

Our friends Mike (Jewish) and Kass (Christian) certainly saw it that way. "Before Mike and I got married we not only agreed on the religion for the kids, but we also literally designated a 'VP of Religion,'" Kass told me. "We agreed that our kids would be raised Jewish, and that Mike would be in charge. We both think it's very important that if you are going to have one dominant religion, there is one person taking the lead." Their businesslike treatment of the matter might have something to do with the fact that they started a company together, but you really can't fault the logic.

And we do know people who didn't really think religion through before marriage, and so are sorting it out after the fact. Take our friends Ben and Allie: They never fight about anything, really, but four years in and thinking about having kids, they are facing the biggest point of contention in their marriage so far, debating whether to join a Catholic or Protestant church.

Still, we've discussed it numerous times, and we don't see the need to commit to any specific plan before we marry. Our view is similar to that of my friend David, a Jewish child of interfaith parents, now married to my friend Lara, who's not Jewish. He describes himself and his wife as "fairly secular people," who are "equally nonstressed" about the issue. He notes that "religion had better not be a fundamental part of your identity" if you want to make an interfaith marriage work. And I think he's right. But if religion were truly a deal-breaker for either of us, we wouldn't be here in the first place. I know at least one couple that was truly, deeply in love but broke it off over religious discrepancies, and many people who deliberately have held themselves back from falling, for similar reasons.

No, the issue here is not solely what Jonathan and I want. It's what the Cohen family wants, too, for their kids and their grandkids, and also for themselves. Enter the need to set boundaries.

The wedding, with its potential for religious themes, is a good trial run in this regard. We quickly realized that it wasn't in our best interest to discuss the content of the ceremony with anyone, period. We took in advice from various parties, but the communication channel only went one way. Our officiant, a retired judge, is going to help us incorporate a few elements traditionally found in Jewish ceremonies, such as breaking a glass. But no one knows that yet, and they won't until the rehearsal. It's our way of saying thanks for the input, but you don't get a vote.

Jonathan's steadfastness with this rule is very heartening, especially because there's no conversion in my future. Despite my zeal for atoning on Yom Kippur, my enthusiastic (but clumsy) adoption of Yiddish phrases, my fondness for bialys and matzoh ball soup, and even my love for a whole family full of Jewish people, foremost among them my husband, I am not Jewish. And I never will be.

It's two-pronged: One, I'll never truly belong to that culture; two, I just can't find a way to believe in organized religion. I was raised Catholic, so I did the CCD-on-Wednesdays thing, and the mass-on-Sunday thing, and I memorized all my prayers like the good girl I was, to the point that they'll still pop into my head in times of trouble. But I do not believe.

I allow that there are forces bigger than myself at work in the universe. I acknowledge the interconnectedness of nearly everything, and notice it more and more every day. I believe that people, both living and dead, can be very wise and tuned in, and that those people's ideas are worthy of study. But I don't think any human being, or any anthropomorphized god, is worthy of worship. My life's commandments are written in my own words.

One thing I do worship, however, is Christmastime. I could leave the rest of the Christian traditions, but come December, I love it all—the trees, the lights, the cookies, the carols, the presents, the crackling fires. To be more specific, though, I love Christmas the way my family does it. (And I couldn't be more thrilled that getting married doesn't mean I'll have to spend every other year with someone else's version.) To me, Christmas is memories: Baking cookies with my aunts when I was little, and, in more recent years, drinking martinis with my brother. It's traditions: the Christmas Eve drive to look at the lights, a different wrapping-paper theme every year, green bean casserole with our turkey. It's rituals: Christmas breakfast with our friends Stacy and Bob; curling up on the couch in new flannel pajamas to watch my dad try on the sweaters my mom bought him, or to watch the cat, a length of satin ribbon looped around her neck, wedge herself into an abandoned gift box, her gut spilling over the sides.

It's also just so . . . *good*, in every sense. I love that Christmas compels people to try harder to care for one another, even if they don't always succeed. Yes, I know that's a sentimental, Frank Capra-esque view of an extremely commercialized holiday. And I like it that way! I grew up feeling sorry for kids who didn't get to roll around in all that Christmas goodness like gluttonous, deranged elves, and I guess I always will. No kid of mine will go without.

So I've begun my campaign, a subtle one, despite my obnoxious zeal for the holiday. Jonathan's already spent one Christmas with us, and pronounced it swell. Recently, as a favor to a friend, I edited a short essay for the liner notes of a homemade Christmas CD. It was about family and ritual, nothing at all about religion, and it made me cry like the big blubbering sap I am. I e-mailed it to Jonathan, telling him that it perfectly captured how I feel.

I'm optimistic. The way we celebrate Christmas at my parents' household, I don't see why our kids couldn't go to Hebrew school, get bar mitzvahed, the whole nine, and still snuggle up in front of the tree. Jonathan's brother Brian once made an interesting point, though. He feels strongly that if a child is given any choice at all, there's no way he or she will choose to side with the minority. That the giant Christmas goose will swallow everything else.

I tend to think that's an overly fearful point of view, and that, as long as dogma is minimized, there's room for an almost limitless number of traditions and celebrations. The more the merrier. But I'm also aware that I'm coming at this from a majority perspective. I've never really been an outsider of any kind. My friend David summed up the "concern with the amount of interfaith marriages occurring amongst American Jewry" as "a fear of extinction, both numbers and culture," and that makes a lot of sense.

It's odd to think of this marriage in that way, as me affiliating myself with a minority, a group with special needs and concerns, and perhaps in need of special protection. I've started to read the paper differently now; to hear people's comments differently. And both because keeping the Jewish culture alive is important to the Cohens, and because, in short order, it will be entrusted to my generation, I'll make an effort not to let any cherished traditions die.

And ultimately, I don't think that what the Cohens desire and what I desire is all that different. Our green bean casserole is their farfel, so to speak. I've had so many big dinners around the Cohen table that the religious festivities blend with the secular and the plain old family celebrations, but the dinner that comes to mind in an instant was in honor, at least in part, of a very special holiday of sorts: Jonathan's grandparents' sixty-eighth wedding anniversary. They're both nearly ninety. Mom Rosie is always impeccably dressed, and, when you least expect it, as quick with a riposte as ever, but she fades in and out. As always, Abba had sent Mom Rosie flowers, which they left at home, but he brought the card to dinner, to read it aloud to the table. He pulled it out of his pocket, put on his glasses, cleared his throat, and read: "I love you always, and in all ways."

His eyes filled with tears. Mine did, too. But Mom Rosie's

face stayed more or less blank. "I don't think she notices it," he added, shaking his head. But we noticed. We heard. We were there to bear witnesses to his effort, to his wit, and to a love that had endured for almost seven decades. Our presence helped him mark the occasion, and helped make it real. As far as something to believe in, all the key elements were there: the family, the traditions, and, most of all, the memories, spanning from one generation to the next.

F WORDS OF WISDOM

If you're embarking on an interfaith marriage, may the Flying Spaghetti Monster bless you. You'll probably need some help at some point along the way. Religious leaders and friends are good sources of advice, but exercise caution when involving your parents. This is just one more moment when what the two of you want is paramount, and it may take some detangling from your "families of origin" to figure out what that really is. Be respectful, of course, but don't be afraid to guard your privacy on this issue.

~

You and your fiancé, however, should be very open with each other. Religion, like kids, demands a thorough dissection and discovery process before you make a lifelong commitment. No matter how small a role religion plays in your life at the moment, allow that people change, and take the time to imagine how you'll feel as your life progresses, and your family grows. Ask your fiancé to do the same. Then talk about it, and make a plan for how you'll handle any disagreements.

~

For more help and ideas, pick up *A Nonjudgmental Guide to Interfaith Marriage* by Steven Carr Reuben, or *Joining Hands and Hearts: Interfaith, Intercultural Wedding Celebrations—A Practical Guide for Couples* by Susanna Stefanachi Macomb. And check out www.beliefnet.com—it has some great resources.

April 7

BE OUR GUESTS

We're inviting who? How? And when? Spreading the word about the wedding does much more than get you on the calendar.

The last invitation has been addressed. Jonathan did most of them—he has nicer handwriting. His mom offered again and again to hire a professional, but I kept declining. I thought it would be a worthwhile meditation to write our guests' names out in longhand letting the list take shape in our minds, like copying out notes before a test.

I'll have to ask Jonathan if he feels prepared.

But it wasn't *that* inequitable, really. I did a good handful. And I think I addressed more of the save-the-dates. That was the more intense part of the invitation process, anyway, because we (sort of) made them ourselves—we printed the text on clear mailing labels and stuck them on the back of postcards—and because that was the moment when this thing, our wedding, really began to take shape.

Typing all those names into the spreadsheet, my life—past, present, and future—was literally lined up in black and white in front of me.

Childhood/high school/college friends. Friends from all my many jobs. People I'd never have met if it weren't for Jonathan; people I "couldn't pick out of a police lineup," as Jonathan puts it, but who will no doubt play a role in our married lives.

> Typing all those names into the spread-sheet, my life—past, present, and future—was literally lined up in black and white in front of me.

In many ways, assembling The List was the most stressful part of the process to date, because that's when we did the heavy negotiating about who's getting invited, and who's not. With our friends, it was fairly obvious, though I did have to talk Jonathan out of some quid pro quo invites. We just can't have that big a wedding. And I swear that people won't be offended—Seinfeld has that bit about how nobody really wants to come to your wedding, anyway, and in many ways I think he's right. My philosophy is that if someone has even one instant of "Why on earth am *I* invited to this?" when he or she tears open the envelope, then that's an invitation wasted.

My ideal guest list would be made up of people who really, truly want to be there, plus the odd date or two (I think it's wrong to invite anyone, no matter who they are, without a "guest," especially if they're traveling to attend) and the blasé teenage cousin. But it's easy to get into the whole "Well, they invited me, so they really must want me there" loop, when you really invited them because "they might feel slighted if we didn't." Instead of that tepid, polite, two-step, wouldn't it be better if you only invited people who would be devastated if they *weren't* there? That's been a useful decision-making tool throughout this whole process: We can do this or that, sure, but can we *not* do it? It's a much stricter standard.

That's wedding planning in a vacuum, though. Every married couple I've ever discussed it with has told me that they wound up with a bigger list than they would have liked. All bets are off when it comes to family on both sides and the in-laws' family friends. I can't possibly know all the back-stories with the people Jonathan's parents want to invite, and so my message to them was "Anyone that you really want to have with you on that day, invite them. It will all work out."

Of course, it helped that as Jonathan's mom gave me more and more names, she kept saying, "Don't worry, they'll never come." That soothing mantra haunts my dreams at night, because if they *do* come, we're screwed. I'm trying to stay positive, because many of the people on their list would have to travel a significant distance to attend. And I also take some comfort in the fact that everybody—airlines, doctors, other brides—overbooks. I've never met a couple that invited fewer people than their venue could hold, and yet I've never heard of such a thing as a wedding guest having to take a bump. (*Sure, I'll give up my seat at table twelve for complimentary bar coupons, room service, and pay-per-view!*) So it must just cosmically come together.

But we are building in some cushion, at the expense of some of our newer friends, and, sadly, my parents. I'm betting that pretty much everyone they invite *will* come, seeing as most of our friends and family live in or around two cities in Nebraska, and the place where we're having the wedding is just up the road a piece. That's why we've got a lopsided list.

And though it took a while to get there, when we finally got that list set, and dropped those save-the-dates in the mailbox, It Was Official. It was "out there." The train had left the station. More than accepting the proposal, showing off the ring, calling friends and family, sending in the deposit for the venue, or anything else, mailing the save-the-dates made me feel like we were really going to do this.

Save-the-dates are a fairly recent innovation, and I think they really up the ante. We sent them out way back in early December, as recommended by Martha Stewart in her clip 'n' save timeline, the one piece of planning material I've been consulting. But they caused a bit of friction between my mother and me, because she isn't completely convinced that they're necessary, largely because they're still pretty rare in her neck of the woods. Many Nebraska weddings still involve mostly Nebraskans, which means less travel, probably fewer scheduling demands, and a generally more laid-back attitude.

In retrospect—and hang onto your veil—I think my mom was right. Though I was passionately convinced that they needed to go out when they did, they probably could have been mailed a month or two later, or even not at all. Maybe the save-the-date is just another succulent piece of wedding-industry baloney that I gobbled right up. Though it did help in terms of venue selection to have a rough idea of how many people we're going to have, if we had skipped the save-the-date and just sent out the invitation a reasonable number of weeks before the wedding, wouldn't the guest list work itself out? Our nearest and dearest had the date on their calendars as soon as we picked it, and as for the others, the people who were meant to be there would be able to make it, and we'd just catch up with the others some other time?

Or—and this sneaky idea is only occurring to me now, as I'm staring at this mammoth pile of invitations—perhaps save-the-dates are most useful for communicating with a certain subset of guests: people who you may not talk to daily, weekly, or even monthly, but who you absolutely know you want to have with you on your wedding day, and who will need to travel long distances to get there.

If I had it to do over, I think I'd take that approach. We didn't do the A-list and B-list thing; we were sort of offended by the concept of breaking our guest list into tiers. But a few things have changed in the past three months, and let's just say that I might compose the list slightly differently if I were putting it together for the first time right now.

On the bright side, it's nice that we had an early opportunity to communicate with our guests, because it was a good way to begin setting the tone of the event. We want the wedding to be really relaxed and fun, not at all formal. The rustic lodge where people are staying and the barn where we're having the ceremony will go a long way toward that, but people won't see their surroundings until they arrive, and so I want to give them some clues about what to expect, and how to dress.

For the save-the-dates, I just bought a mixed bag of post-cards with linoleum-block prints of various flora and fauna—frogs, raccoons, chickadees, violets, dandelions, mushrooms, and more—from Gwen Frostic Prints, in northern Michigan. My friend Lori, whose family has a summer home in the area, turned me on to Gwen Frostic years ago, and her stuff is still my paper product of choice for most every occasion. Gwen herself died some years back, but her family maintains her little wood-land shop with an equal spirit of wonder and joy at the privilege of sharing this planet with other creatures. And they sell on the Internet. So whenever Manhattan gets to be too much for me, I log on and buy some notecards festooned with birch trees and maple leaves. Their postcards are perfect for the kind of wed-ding we're trying to create. Coupled with the obvious DIY efforts of our clear mailing labels, and the Web site we point people to (www.nebraskanuptials.com, which we chose for comic, alliterative effect, and which our friend Jen designed with rustic flair), I think the save-the-dates did a good job of conveying the spirit we're bringing to the wedding. And they were easy enough to put together and send out.

The invitations themselves were a slightly different story. Jonathan's dad is a dentist, and he's been bartering his services for years. He built up an enormous credit at Beverly's, a sta-tionery store in their hometown. It was very generous of the Cohens to let us use it, and we wound up with gorgeous, deca-dent letterpress in spring green and black on thick, creamy stock. Lynn even gave me an enormous head start on finding the right manufacturer, spending what I'm sure was a considerable amount of time looking through designs with Beverly of Beverly's, and making suggestions about which enormous books to pull down from the shelves when I finally went to look at a store in New York. Lynn had homed in on my taste and narrowed the field so well that I found a wonderful design—gracefully arching ferns on the invitation; taut, curly fiddleheads on the response card and some thank-you notes—in less than five minutes.

Once we had picked the design, Jonathan and I sat down to write the text. We wanted to acknowledge the fact that everybody's chipping in financially, but avoid a long list of names; skip any fusty British spellings; and shear off any notes of formality that didn't work with the casual vibe we're trying to foster. We also wanted to be classy and not horrify any of our older relatives. It's not an easy task, since every word on a wedding invitation is thick with meaning, but because we're both writers, I'm sure it took us a lot less time than it could have. I was ecstatic that he and I agreed on how it should read, and on the fact that we'd write it first, and get our parents' signoff second.

So it was with a light heart that I e-mailed our text to Beverly . . . and with seething rage that I pulled the dummy layout off the fax machine a few days later. Middle names had been inserted! It said "marriage" instead of "wedding"! They had spelled out the date and time, and added the dreaded "o'clock"! It said "honour"!!!

I realized that while I thought I was handing in final copy—

as any editor would—Beverly thought that I was submitting material for a lively debate between her and Emily Post. It made me irrationally angry. After some rather heated back and forth, we reached a compromise, and I'm happy with the way they look. But I'm still amazed by my vehement reaction. I guess I needed to dig my heels in and prevent other people from tarting up my humble, simple wedding invitation because, well, I didn't want anyone to get the wrong idea about what we're doing here. If there's a more public place than the wedding invitation to say "I'm sticking with tradition" or "I'm doing things differently," I'm not sure where it is.

The wounds from that battle of wills flared up when the invitations arrived—looking perfect, thank goodness—and it was time to address the envelopes. While Jonathan followed his mom's advice for her list, addressing them to, say, "Dr. and Mrs. McDreamy," I took a different approach. For our friends, and for my parents' list, I dropped the salutation altogether, and, when it felt right, put the woman's name first. So there.

There were other little decisions I made along the way that came so naturally that I didn't even think about them at the time—like the fact that we had both our names and our address printed on the response card envelopes and the backs of the other envelopes, which practically screamed "WE'RE LIVING IN SIN!"

Oh, well, too late to do anything about that. And now that all is said and done, and the goods are stacked up in their neat little vanilla-colored piles, I'm feeling calm, like we've accomplished something. From my perspective, at least, we've successfully bridged various people's expectations and desires, accommodating both tradition and personal preference.

So I guess our woodsy wedding-to-be is in the clear . . . until we have to tackle the place cards and the seating chart.

F WORDS OF WISDOM

Consider whether you really need save-the-dates. If you decide you do, consider sending them only to family and close friends who will need to make advance travel arrangements.

~

Don't be surprised if the look, cost, or phrasing of the save-the-dates and/or invitations are a major point of contention among the various parties invested in the wedding. People who run stationery shops witness jaw-dropping battles. After all, it is the first moment when everyone has to come together and agree on a public declaration about the look, feel, and tone of the event. Plus there seems to be a lot of intergenerational strife on this one: brides and grooms prefer more casual; their parents would go more traditional.

~

In composing your list, think about things that might change in between now and your wedding day. Co-workers are probably the trickiest decisions to make. Other than people with whom you socialize outside of work, you probably should invite your direct boss, and anyone who reports to you directly. Or just apply the ultimate rule of thumb, for all social circles: If you'd be sad or miffed if you weren't invited to their wedding, make sure they're invited to yours. Another tip: If you're debating whether to invite someone, think about where you'd seat him or her at the reception. If you can't think of where that person would fit in, perhaps that's your answer right there.

~

Buying a clever URL for your wedding Web site, especially if you are planning to use it as a major way to communicate with your guests, can make it easier for people to remember. Something with both your names is more common, but can be confusing. (Was it Brad-Angelina.com? Angelina-Brad.com? Brangelina.com?) It's also more fun to have your own URL instead of using whatever the Knot spits out for you.

April 16

COURTSHIP INTERRUPTUS

It's sinking in: We're going to play these roles for the rest of our lives . . . with no script, and no Hollywood endings.

A COUPLE MORNINGS AGO, I tossed and turned for hours, not sleeping, but refusing to open my eyes, trying to keep consciousness at bay. When Jonathan finally rolled over, slid out of bed, and stretched, I went silent and motionless, letting the dread cover me like a heavy blanket, pushing me deeper into the layer between sleep and waking.

"Kel. Wake up."

When I finally pulled myself to the surface, I saw Jonathan by the side of the bed, freshly showered and looking stricken, cradling something in his palm.

"I accidentally knocked it off the counter with my towel," he said. "I'm sorry."

The porcelain brooch, a spray of wild pink roses with pale yellow centers, was in four or five pieces, its paper-thin petals a mass of ragged, spiky edges.

I looked in his eyes. Neither of us knew what to say.

This was a twist.

We'd been fighting on and off for about a week—and not just about pet peeves and household annoyances. Most nights we'd fall asleep in the permafrost, a canyon of ice between our bodies in the queen-size bed, hence my reluctance to wake up and face the deadly chill. But that day, instead of the anger and silence I had feared, morning brought this bizarre accident, with all the qualities of a portentous dream.

> Most nights we'd fall asleep in the permafrost, a canyon of ice between our bodies in the queen-size bed.

The brooch wasn't an heirloom or anything, or at least not my family's heirloom. I bought it last summer at the flea market on Avenue A from the woman who's sold me many a 1950s plastic necklace. But it was pretty and absurdly delicate, and I loved to marvel at it, if not to wear it that often. It had recently occurred to me to ask my hairstylist if she could wire it to a barrette and tuck it into my wedding-day up-do. So I had taken it out of the top drawer of the old white bureau that serves as both storage and counter space in our bathroom, and placed it on top, among the lotion and deodorant bottles and piles of other jewelry, so I could glance at it while getting ready, and visualize how it might look in my hair, complement my dress.

Now it was shattered.

All I could think was, "Did we really just mail all those invitations?"

The honeymoon, way before it's scheduled to begin, is undeniably over.

The torrent of mix CDs he made me faithfully every couple of weeks before we got engaged, one of his primary ways of wooing me, has dried to a trickle. Romantic dinners—and sex—are on the decline.

It's almost a cliché. Even Jonathan's mom has joked about it. "What does a bride do in bed?" she asked on a note accompanying a gift of stationery. "Write thank-you notes, of course."

And I can't say we weren't warned. Back in the fall, during our marriage ed courses, it was a recurring theme. "The big mistake that couples make is that when they start living together, they stop dating," said Patty, from Marriage Success Training. She also made that comment about the risk of cheating being higher, because your bond isn't yet "cemented." Cement seems an apt metaphor right now: dull, gray, hardening, a trap. The challenges of this process and our relentless proximity can be a deadly combination. Instead of primping separately and meeting each other for a drink looking perfect, I watch him stare in the mirror, obsessing about his hairline, while he hears me sneeze repeatedly as I apply my mascara, then curse when it inevitably smudges. There's a certain warmth and security in sharing these mundane things, but at the same time we're eroding the polish that we carefully layered on while we were courting each other. And then there are the bigger things. We're here when the other person comes back from the doctor's appointment, opens the credit card bill, and gets the late-night phone call from home, or the unbidden text message from a red-flag number. We're here to watch how the other person handles all of the above. We're here for every such thing, and we'll always be here. In all these actions and reactions, we can't escape it: This is the person I'm marrying.

Honestly, though, I never actually tire of having him around, a fact that I find heartening, and surprising, especially since we share such a small apartment. This isn't about wanting less of him. But I do have a sense that, even if I'm not consciously acknowledging it, I might benefit from a little more time just for me.

Not long ago, a writer friend was doing a newspaper column on "single envy," and looking for anecdotes. "Don't pretend you don't know what I'm talking about," she wrote in a group e-mail. "Even those of us in blissful coupletude occasionally find ourselves envious of our single friends. They seem thinner, don't they? And they wear better clothes. They are always going out and meeting new people and going to parties or, like, cultural events, and if they stay home, well, they can watch whatever they want on TV."

Of course, I hit Reply:

I miss privacy, and time to just be. It sounds stupid, but there are times when I feel like the parent of a small child who can't get enough time alone. Whether he's knocking on the door while I'm in the bathtub or frowning at me for smoking a cigarette on the balcony, I'm acutely aware that he figures into all my decisions now, and will forever. . . . Then again, when he's making me dinner, or doing my laundry, or picking up the slack in our joint lives in one of the many little ways that make a huge difference, I'm glad to give up some of that solitude.

Then I hit Send.

I *am* glad to give up that solitude. But I'm also loathe to lose the "single stuff." And that's not just about eating ice cream by myself on the couch, or going out on dates—with one guy or a succession of guys. It's also about not being yoked to anyone. Being able to just throw up my hands and walk away when the going gets tough.

That used to be my favorite means of escape. In a lot of ways, I thought that wanting to marry someone meant that I'd never want to walk away again. That getting engaged meant we'd want to find a way to work through everything, together. But even in our brief time dating and being engaged, there have been times when we just don't want anything to do with each other, and so I've found myself asking the question, "Is there something wrong with us?" While there's a lot that's beautiful about this process, I'm discovering that there's plenty of ugly stuff mixed in!

> In a lot of ways, I thought that wanting
> to marry someone meant that I'd never
> want to walk away again. But even in
> our brief time dating and being engaged,
> there have been times when we just
> don't want anything to do with each
> other, and so I've found myself asking
> the question, "Is there something wrong
> with us?"

Why that's surprising to me, I don't know, because life is full of ugly stuff, so why would this particular time get special dispensation? Plus, shouldn't I, as a relationship writer, be able to see right through all these damaging engagement-and-wedding myths about romance and perfection and champagne-colored clouds?

But that's the punchline: I can't. Turns out that my preconceived ideas about how this time in Jonathan and my life should work, look, and feel are as deeply rooted as anyone else's. That realization came galloping home at breakneck speed while I prepped for a recent appearance on the *Today* show, with an author I've mentioned, Allison Moir-Smith, who wrote that delightful book about why your engagement isn't necessarily the happiest time of your life. I knew I'd only have time for a few quick soundbites, and that my time probably would be better spent buying the right outfit and getting my hair highlighted than by writing a speech. But I wanted to get my thoughts together, to try to distill my gut reaction to being engaged into something concise and coherent. I wound up with six pages of notes, in a furious scrawl, on the subject of Why Our Over-Romanticizing of Engagements (Plus Lots of Other Cultural Factors) Sets Women Up for Disillusionment, Disappointment, and Distress.

I discovered that I was angry about a lot of things, astonished by other things, perplexed by many more. I was pissed off about the push/pull number that society does on engaged women—be flawless on your wedding day, but don't you dare act like a monster! About the fact that we get so much pressure to go this route in the first place: *Gotta get married, gotta have a wedding, gotta make it perfect.* It's no more possible to be "perfect" on your wedding day than on any other, and yet we're obsessed with the idea of perfection, from the way you look, to the kind of party you throw, to how you feel, or, more accurately, *appear to* feel. (How unfair is that? What is Bridezilla if not a woman striving for the "perfect" wedding, pushed to the brink?)

I scribbled on and on about how being engaged is like a secret society: You don't even really know it exists until you're in it. Or, rather, you're aware of "it," but you have little more than a whole lot of misinformation about what "it" is. And once you're inducted, you're liable to think that you're the only bride who's feeling the way you do, unless you're lucky enough to

> What is Bridezilla if not a woman
> striving for the "perfect" wedding,
> pushed to the brink?

have a close, candid friend who's gone through it recently—or, even luckier, to have observed her planning said wedding with your own eyes. It seems to me that people get Engagement Amnesia, only recalling the good parts. Revisionist history serves its purpose, mental-health wise, but it's too bad for our culture that the traumatic parts of people's engagements, if not erased from memory altogether, don't often get shared.

Even my Aunt Carrie, one of the smartest people I know, and one of the most given to reflection and self-analysis—not to mention honesty and caring—sent me a card, when Jonathan and I got engaged, telling me to "enjoy this fun time." Then at my Nebraska shower, mere weeks before the wedding, she told me that she and my uncle Dan (now married for more than twenty years, with two teenage daughters), had such a big fight

> Being engaged is like a secret society:
> You don't even really know it exists until
> you're in it.

the night before the wedding that she remembers thinking, "Let's get this over with quickly so I can begin divorce proceedings." (At that same shower, I also learned that, on her wedding day, I had looked at Carrie and said, quite seriously, "Well, it's not too late to change your mind." I was her flower girl, and seven years old.)

I wrote all about that paradox. Then I vented about how unhappiness during your engagement is extra disconcerting, seeing as you took this giant step precisely *because* you and hubby-to-be felt so connected and ready. So when the trouble hits—BAM!—it's like one of those asinine free-fall rides at a carnival, the ones that take you way up high and then just drop the bottom out. (And in the moment, it's such a dramatic shift that it's difficult to step back and see that the process probably is more like a Ferris wheel, part of a cycle that will come back around.)

Finally, I tore into wedding planning. Throughout our engagement, I've been experiencing bouts of what I'm calling Inequality Rage—utter indignation that no matter how enlightened we think we are, or try to be, much, much more of the burden of planning this wedding is falling on me than it is on Jonathan. It's just how it is. Somehow, women are the only sex that knows how to wrap gifts. Likewise, women plan weddings. End of story.

So that's what I expounded on, at great length, in my little blue notebook. But what did I actually wind up *saying* on the *Today* show? Nothing of much consequence: "It's different than how society wants you to think it is, but it's great, it's still great!"

And when Natalie Morales tried to make it personal—"So, what did you learn about your fiancé that you didn't know before you got engaged?"—ha. Like I was falling for that one.

But that's why books are better than television, right?

Before we went live that morning, I sat there on that couch in the cold studio under all the bright lights, watching the opening montage on the small screen, seeing all the photographs I had e-mailed to the producer flashing one by one on the screen. Jonathan and me walking across the Brooklyn Bridge. Camping upstate. Mugging for the camera at my friend Mary's wedding. Steady smiles, steady postures, the same embrace over and over again—a collection of high points, which only tell half the story. Not an accurate reflection of what this has really been: not a free-fall ride, not a Ferris wheel, and, no, not even bumper cars. It's been a roller-coaster.

I thought about the show a lot over the course of the day Jonathan woke me to say he'd broken my pin. Clearly we were both thinking, and softening, scared straight by what had happened: by my cold anger in that moment, by his remorse, by the fact that bad things are going to happen to us, and we are going to cause each other pain, and we are simply going to have to find a way to deal with it, and move on. We chatted on IM. Made plans for the evening. I didn't ask Jonathan to try to get the pin fixed, but I secretly hoped he would, and that it could be fixed, and look fine, and be all the better for having been broken and mended again, a fine metaphor for what we've endured.

Indeed, without saying anything about it beforehand, Jonathan had taken the broken brooch to the jewelry shop down the street, the same one where he bought my engagement ring. But I didn't get my happy ending.

"Don't bother," the man at the shop told him. "It would cost way more to fix it than the pin is worth."

It's no matter. The more I think about it, the more I think it wouldn't have worked in my hair, anyway—much too heavy and cumbersome. And now I have one less thing to fuss over, one less fragile thing to pack. Something to let go of. In time, the breaking of the pin will probably come to feel fated, inevitable. The cold bathroom tile. The delicate porcelain. The fight.

As far as the ultimate outcome, though, I'm not superstitious. Why start now? I'm glad that he made the effort to try and get it fixed. That's enough for me. It makes it easier to look at the pieces, which I doubt I'll ever bring myself to throw away. They're still pretty to look at, after all. And yes, they'll remind me that our relationship isn't unbreakable, that it needs to be handled with care—and that even during the jagged patches, it's something worth hanging onto.

F Words of Wisdom

Allow for ebbs and flows in every kind of emotion during your engagement—including how fondly you think of your fiancé.

~

If you feel like you are doing all the wedding work, you probably are. Equality is an ongoing struggle. But do the best you can to involve your fiancé—the patterns you establish now will carry over into your marriage.

~

Do try to be engaged for at least a year. No, it doesn't take a year to plan a wedding, but it can take that long to get used to the fact that you are getting married, and to do all the emotional work that pops up along the way. And do not let the planning itself expand to fill every moment of that year. Concentrate on yourself and your feelings, and on your fiancé as a fiancé and not as a boyfriend or a husband. Don't be afraid to take the time you need, even if other forces are pushing you forward—even if it means putting on the brakes and postponing the wedding. You won't be the first couple in the history of the world to do so. Or the last.

April 25

PARTY POLITICS

Making the "bachelorette" more than a necessary evil.

WHEN IT'S BACHELORETTE-PARTY TIME, that means you're in the home stretch, right? It's time to relax, kick back, have fun, and reap the real rewards of being a bride. Sure, that's true. Except when it's not. Except when memories of all the horrifying, or just plain boring, bachelorette parties you've attended—or bumped into at bars—start flickering through your mind on a reel to a slasher-movie soundtrack, and you begin living in dread of what might transpire at yours.

I've always liked the idea of giving a person—male or female—a sendoff from single life, and the ridiculous sex stuff doesn't really bother me. But bachelorette parties are typically much more conspicuous than their male equivalents, and much sillier, and that's what really irks me. I became even more embarrassed by them after getting engaged, just knowing that there was a feather boa out there with my name on it—to say nothing of far more frightening accessories.

> Bachelorette parties are typically much
> more conspicuous than their male equiv-
> alents, and much sillier.

I knew that my friends more or less knew how I felt, and therefore wouldn't do anything too awful, but they also wouldn't dream of skipping the statutory celebration. I suppose if I had explicitly forbade it, they'd have obeyed. But that's not my style. I sort of wish it were; wish I were better at saying no to the parts of getting married that make me uncomfortable. But given that ever-present risk of appearing ungracious, or spoiling other people's fun, I'm realizing that it helps to just give in, at least a little, to being public property.

It also helps to try to tap into the feeling-loved thing. To realize that even if they don't do it just the way I would, and even if it's a little embarrassing, the people around me are trying to celebrate me. Embracing that fact feels pretty good. Great, even. There is nothing quite like the feeling that someone is planning a party for you, especially when you're in the midst of planning something on the magnitude of a wedding. Eventually, I was able to enjoy the anticipation, enjoy knowing that at some point in this busy, taxing process, somebody else would take the reins and throw a party on my behalf.

Also—and who am I kidding?—most people get a jolt out of a little harmless hazing, and I'm no exception. I've mentioned that I was in a sorority. My high school could have been the prototype for the "abuse the freshman" tactics employed in *Dazed and Confused*. So I know that borderline-humiliating initiation rites stimulate some sadism-lite pleasure center in the brain, that it's all in good fun, and that nobody likes a wet blanket. And I think that's more or less what we're dealing with in the modern bachelorette party. Because I have hazed—I will own up to wielding a penis straw or two in my day—it is my turn to be hazed.

As anticipated, my hazers were quite merciful. I had the most fun, caring, creative, decidedly un-bachelorette-y "bachelorette" day ever, organized by my bridesmaids Joanne and Allie. It began with bouquets of flowers, then proceeded to brunch, yoga, and pedicures at an organic, nontoxic salon, followed by cocktails at a private table, gifts of lacy underthings, a tapas dinner with plenty of sangria, and several bars. It even had a touch of the traditional, without going over the top.

We *did*:

○ Pass around a pack of "52 Outrageous Bachelorette Dares!" cards and halfheartedly try to execute some of them.

○ Play a very clever "how well do you know your fiancé" game that Allie cooked up, with Jonathan's help, of course.

○ Buy a pack of cigarettes and smoke them while gabbing on the sidewalk, randomly bumping into my friend

Joyce's boyfriend in the process. (This is, after all, New York City.)

○ Fall down into a heap while trying to take a photo.

We did *not*:

○ Set foot in one of New York's notorious bachelorette factories—no '80s dance music, body shots, male revues, or cross-dressing waitresses.

○ Brandish one bit of penis paraphernalia. (Unless you count the tiny penis confetti Joanne had artfully scattered on the cocktail table. It was innocuous, though. Suitable for a baby shower, even.)

We wound down the evening salsa-dancing with strange men in a body-to-body club, sweating and sloshing mojitos and grinning like idiots. After a three A.M. nightcap at a diner, with Cokes and mozzarella sticks and disco fries, we pronounced the evening a raging success.

The next day, Jonathan returned from his own last hurrah, a weekend in his old college town. We had timed it so our descents into debauchery would coincide. His was even more elaborate than mine, and, I imagine, less wholesome. I don't have a lot of information about it, except that he wound up hog-tied on top of a pool table at some point. There's a DVD full of photos from his weekend sitting within arm's reach as I type, and I'm only mildly curious.

What I do know is that he had an unforgettably good time, and describes his party in much the same way I talk about mine. Granted, girls don't often scavenge room service off of other people's discarded trays at five A.M.; boys don't usually give each other underwear. We are distinct creatures, and, for the umpteenth time in this process, I'm reminded of that fact. But we both experienced the best outcome of the bachelor/bachelorette party: feeling appreciated, celebrated, and loved.

It did help, though, that I'd had a dry run before my "official" bash. A couple months earlier, I went to my friend Meredith's lakeside, log-cabin childhood home for a girls' weekend with five other friends from college—the Blue House girls, after the off-campus house we shared our senior year. Heading into the weekend, I suspected that there might be a bachelorette-type event on the horizon, and steeled myself to be a good sport. Turns out they went very easy on me: The first night of the trip, they plopped me down on a stool in the kitchen, gave me a tablet of "bad girl" Mad-Libs and that ubiquitous fluffy pink feather boa, and made me dinner. We ate, drank wine, and opened presents, and I ended that evening feeling full, drunk, and, yes, extremely loved.

The official occasion for the reunion was our thirtieth birthdays, but we were really multitasking, squeezing in a reunion, the bachelorette party, and an assignment—a roundtable discussion about how our love lives have changed since we were in college—for *Tango*. We realized that, for the first time, every single one of us was in a long-haul, big-deal relationship. We had two marrieds, two engageds, and three long-term seriouses.

But we also had no kids among us, no one who wasn't drinking because of a baby on the way. It was a heady moment, all of us poised in more or less the same place on similar paths going more or less the same direction. In a group of seven friends, that kind of coordination is rare.

Of course, how we got there varied wildly, which is the special genius of this group. We're similar, but not too much so. We're constantly surprising and delighting each other. We enjoy each other's company perhaps a bit too much, as evidenced by the inane ways we spent our time that weekend: plucking out each other's gray hairs, squishing into one tiny bedroom to play charades, trying on some seriously hideous bridesmaids' dresses someone found buried in a closet, walking in the rain, tooling around town in a giant minivan. They were variations on the things we'd done together in college; a reminder of our enduring ability to amuse each other.

At some point during the weekend, Meredith pointed out a photo on the dresser in the master bedroom. It was of her mother, who passed away not too long ago, with a big group of girlfriends. Their posture and facial expressions looked very, very familiar.

Late Saturday afternoon, we ventured out to her dad's country club, and bellied up to the bar. We were quite a force, the seven of us; rowdy and boozy and talking to the bartender and the television and one another all at once. Gradually, we began to realize that we were getting curious looks from the other patrons. It's sad, but true, that a group of seven thirty-year-old women out having a rip-roaring good time in the middle of the afternoon is a rarity. Eventually, a well-preserved, well-dressed older woman ventured over to say hello. "You remind me of my granddaughter and her friends," she told us. "It's such a pleasure to see you all here together."

> We had a golden opportunity to luxuriate in our friendship, and we were going for it, with unfettered, unself-conscious joy.

That was the first moment I really got it—the bachelorette thing, or its essence, at least. Were we conspicuous? Yes. Silly? Most definitely. But that's because we had a golden opportunity to luxuriate in our friendship, and we were going for it, with unfettered, unselfconscious joy. I guess bounty like that can seem embarrassing—from the outside. But when you're in the inner circle, it feels amazing.

F WORDS OF WISDOM

Schedule your bachelor and bachelorette events for the same/day weekend, so no one gets lonely or has excess fodder for jealousy.

~

Not everyone is self-conscious about being a bachelorette, and that's a good thing. However you feel, your friends should respect your wishes. It's the one place where you should be unafraid to pull rank, because, bottom line, it's the one part of this process that really is all about you. All that "It's your day!" stuff about the wedding—not entirely true. But the bachelorette party most definitely belongs to the bride. Unless you love surprises, speak up about what you want.

~

Don't be afraid to buck the crowd. Just because the standard bachelorette package (ha!) involves tons of plastic penis gadgets, fruity drinks, and, quite likely, oiled-up male flesh, doesn't mean you have to partake—and it doesn't mean that sort of thing is really all that fun. Nor is it cheap, so do your friends a favor if your wishes trend away from the corny stuff—let them know. Most people who hire a stripper spend months trying to erase the memory; most people who get showered with pretty lingerie spend months looking fabulous at bedtime.

~

It's easy to see too little of your friends during your engagement. Relish the bachelorette! And thank everyone who attended profusely, in writing, whether or not they gave you a gift.

May 3

THE DRESS QUEST

What if you can't find something that fits your Inner Bride?

T HOUGH HE'S ADAMANT about not seeing it until the wedding, Jonathan got very emotional the day I went to try on my dress for the first time.

I, on the other hand, wasn't quite feeling it, at least not in the way most people seem to. All that stuff about seeing yourself in your dress and finally being able to visualize yourself as a bride felt like a lot of hype to live up to, and I didn't want to put too much pressure on that first glimpse in the mirror.

> All that stuff about seeing yourself in your dress and finally being able to visualize yourself as a bride felt like a lot of hype to live up to.

In large part, I was cautious because I had no idea what to expect—to that point, the dress had been a wad of fabric, then an idea, then a sketch, then a potato-sack-like creation cut from rough, custard-colored muslin. Nothing even approximating the real thing, that "wow" moment you're supposed to have when you find "the" dress.

My friends and co-workers Elise and Marnie came with me to the shop, partly to support me, and partly, I suspect, because they too were curious to see if it would turn out anything like my vision. "I was pretty nervous about it," Marnie confessed later. "A wedding dress is a pretty big thing to take a risk like that with. What if it hadn't looked anything like you wanted it to?"

When I got there, the shop assistant handed me a bouquet of daisies. "A strange man dropped these off for you," she said, smiling.

Then, at dinner that night, Jonathan said something very sweet: "Talking with you about your ideas about weddings and rings and wedding dresses and all that made me a little nervous as I was getting ready to ask you to marry me. I've glad you've been able to find a way to participate in this that works for you."

It's hard to convey how much that meant to me. I hadn't realized that he had been paying attention to my bitching about the pointlessness and oppressive nature of certain traditions, or to my renegade quest for a dress that felt like me. And his comment helped me realize that my desire to have a wedding dress designed and custom made was my way of turning the costume—and the role—of "bride" into something I could wear comfortably.

> My desire to have a wedding dress
> designed and custom-made was my way
> of turning the costume—and the role—
> of "bride" into something I could wear
> comfortably.

From my earliest forays into wedding-dress shopping, I'd had the powerful feeling that I just didn't want one. They seemed heavy and cumbersome and expensive, and I hated the idea of trying on even one of the samples trapped in thick, smelly vinyl, or worse, hanging limply on the racks, slightly dingy and frayed, even in the nicest of shops. They depressed me.

This was an odd reaction for me, because I'm a vintage clothing fanatic, and an avid wearer of all things used, thrift store, and hand-me-down. I haven't always felt that way. As a child, I was reluctant to even touch the (in retrospect) very nice items that my mom would cherry-pick for me during her volunteer shifts at the Junior League thrift store.

But lately, my mom wishes I didn't like used clothing quite so much. I put together whole outfits from thrift stores and eBay, and crow about my purchases to anyone who will listen. It's not just the price, either: I love the workmanship, the history, the pre-owned feel, the fact that the garment was made and worn and loved years, even decades, before I was born. I'm rarely as excited by a new purchase as I am a vintage one, my engagement ring being a prime example. It had a whole life, or maybe several, before it entered mine. Owning it makes me feel like the guardian of other people's secrets.

But for some reason, when it came to my wedding dress, pre-owned was out of the question. Ditto for anything new but off-the-rack, it seemed, since I kept popping into shops around the city but never was able to bring myself to try anything on. I started to wonder if it was because no matter how new and crisp my actual dress would be, it wouldn't be singular. Someone somewhere else would be wearing that same style, sooner or later, and that felt wrong.

I started to suspect that I might never be satisfied with a dress that hadn't been made for me and me alone. I've heard that every bride has a "thing," something they obsess about to a ridiculous degree. Maybe this is mine.

So I set aside the dress question for a while. Then, on a whim, and as I mentioned before, I decided to look for fabric in Paris while vacationing with two college friends. I picked a random store out of a hotel magazine, showed up, and fought my way through a crowd of tiny Japanese women in Chanel suits to get to the shelves I was looking for. I stared open-mouthed at the bolts and bolts of lace until a large, pushy salesclerk swooped in. I explained what I was looking for in awkward French—I had been practicing the phrase "robe du marriage" on the walk over. I asked for enough fabric for a simple wedding dress, for me, to the floor, no train, no veil. I pointed to three or four bolts, but she pulled down only one. She unfurled it with a flourish. "*Ici. Pour une jeune femme.*" Evidently my other choices were inappropriate. Who am I to argue with a Frenchwoman on matters of taste? My friend Sara and I looked at each other. A mother and daughter nearby argued loudly over mountains of spangled, cream-colored cloth. The room felt very small, and hot. I gave the nod. The saleswoman sized me up, cut the fabric to suit, and I walked out the door with the most expensive clothing purchase of my life hanging from the tip of my finger in a small white shopping bag.

When I got back to New York, I was excited about the lace, though I still had no idea whether it would work. I had no real design in mind. I had no one to make the dress. It was, unquestionably, the most cavalier nonrefundable purchase I had ever made. But I refused to panic, telling myself that it was just crazy enough to *have* to eventually work out perfectly. I turned back people's exclamations of "Wow, that was brave!" with a breezy "It'll either be a wedding dress or heinously expensive curtains!"

Trying to maintain that Zen attitude, I embarked on a search for a designer. I imagined that I'd probably wind up at some fetid, cramped tailor's shop in deep Brooklyn, trying to keep costs down. But again, in an example of the breathtaking simplicity life can offer when you let it, I found my answer a block and a half from my apartment.

It's funny to watch women walk by wedding-dress shops, which, in New York, are fairly plentiful in neighborhoods like mine, thick with all manner of boutiques. Some glance longingly, some stop and stare, and some pound straight by as if they're wearing blinders. I suspect the last group of willfully trying not to look, because that's how I used to be, pre-engagement. Same with wedding magazines—single-girl porn. I suppose it was a combination of embarrassment at my desire, intimidation, and a barely acknowledged fear that I might jinx myself. Want something too much, and it may never be yours. When I first started shopping, before the stores and the dresses started to repulse me, I had the same sort of "you don't belong here" feeling, a residual timidity that was tough to shake.

But I had never felt that way about Adrienne's, a shop I've walked by almost every day since I moved into Jonathan's apartment. With soft pink walls and a good variety of interesting dresses in the window, it always seemed friendly. I made an appointment, and walked in with the lace and some vague ideas. The owner, Gina, immediately began to sketch a design. When I walked out with several pieces of crisp white paper covered with elegant pencil drawings, I started to feel I was onto something.

I shopped around a little more, but eventually made another appointment at Adrienne's, and brought a bunch of my bridesmaids. Finally, I tried on dresses, things that were similar to the idea that was beginning to form, on paper, and in my head. I couple days later I came back one last time, asked them to make a couple alterations to my favorite sketch, then plunked down a deposit.

From there, the process got more and more exciting. It was fun to run down the stairs and out the door to visit my dress. I especially liked the draping, back in the muslin stage. Watching Gina, her big pregnant stomach poking out of a black tank top, crouch down in her red-and-black Nike high tops to inspect the hem, then straighten to trim a new neckline, shearing the fabric straight off my body, and pin on more strips of cloth to fashion the sleeve just so, I saw the dress being built before my eyes. My mom was in town the day we did the draping, and she remarked that it looked as if Gina was sculpting. Gina told us that she *was* a sculptor, an art major in college, who got her dressmaker's training in her mother's shop.

Best of all, that first "real" fitting didn't disappoint, and not just because I had kept my expectations low. The dress wasn't anywhere near finished, of course. I had to undo a row of pins to get into it, and imagine a finished, scalloped hem, and key-hole back, and cap sleeves, and the modest godet in the skirt we decided to add at the last minute, to provide a little flounce and swirl. So I didn't get that jolt of bridal recognition—and I probably won't, until I put it on the day of the wedding. But I did get something more subtle and complex, that warm rush of accomplishment and relief you feel when you know you've helped create something beautiful, and that it's going to meet your expectations.

Now we're almost at the end. I just had my second-to-last fitting. I walked into the boutique to see Gina, her fifteen-day-old daughter, and her husband, who owns the guitar shop across the street, snuggling on the settee amid a forest of white dresses. As Gina pinned me, I noticed that the whites of her eyes were still red from the blood vessels she popped during her twenty-four-hour labor. She and her staff have worked so hard to make me a perfect dress—a dress that is perfect for me, that is, from the style, to the fit, to the spirit in which it was assembled. The gradual nature of this process has been perfect, too. The dress has evolved along with me, both of us getting ready, stage by stage, for showtime.

I'm glad that Jonathan, who had his suit made, got to have a similar experience. I don't think I could bear seeing him in a rented tux. A rented anything on your wedding day seems wildly inadequate. No matter now good it looks, it can't be very high quality, and it will never be a keepsake. Jonathan's parents feel the same way, and helped us figure out how to get him appropriately kitted out. We went to a tailor in his hometown, who made him a beautiful Egyptian cotton shirt, but we ended up at Brooks Brothers for the suit itself, because they had more fabric choices. We cheaped out a little, though—the poor groom generally does get the shaft in this process—and skipped the by-hand custom option in favor of their "digital tailoring" service. The tailoring itself is done by hand, of course, but they use a newfangled means of measuring you. Jonathan stripped down to his boxers and stepped into a tiny booth for a full-body scan, which resulted in a hilarious *Blade Runner*-esque printout, and a fascinatingly detailed list of dimensions. (I am *never* stepping into one of those booths.)

Despite that wacky, futuristic technology, there's something wonderfully old-fashioned about how we've assembled our wedding clothes. I've even felt disappointed with the parts of our outfits that couldn't be made by hand. For example, I had an extremely hard time finding wedding shoes. Though there is a place in Manhattan where you can learn to cobble your own shoes, I restrained myself. But I did try to find other ways around the need for white satin uglies. I thought I had scored when I bought a pair of brushed bronze leather heels at a little Brazilian boutique. But everyone who saw them with the dress agreed that they didn't quite work. After many hours of online research, I wound up at MyGlassSlipper.com. The name is repulsive, but I did find some kick-ass white shoes there. They look great with the dress, but I imagine a far better second life for them, dyed chartreuse or vermilion or some other scandalously bright color.

The rings, too, were a compromise between ready-made and custom. We bought Jonathan's from a store in New York's diamond district that I love, 1,873 Unusual Wedding Rings. It seemed a bit much to custom-make a ring for someone who's never worn a piece of jewelry in his life, and besides, with that much selection, how could he not find something perfect? I think he would have happily worn about three-quarters of their massive inventory.

Finding my ring has taken much longer. I must be growing more comfortable with this getting-married thing, because I can finally visualize myself wearing something that says "married," and wearing it on my ring finger. I've seen a style of eternity band I like, three rows of tiny white diamonds, pave set in yellow gold, at a few stores, including Tiffany's. So there's a jeweler in Jonathan's hometown, who, after a few false starts, is working on something similar. (I hope. I've been informed that I won't be seeing it until it gets slipped on my finger during the ceremony.)

I love the idea that, on our wedding day, we'll both be

putting on carefully handmade clothes. I also like that our ring fingers, both naked at the moment, will be getting dressed at the same time. I think that, to borrow a phrase from Men's Wearhouse, we're gonna love the way we look.

But it's not just about externals. Sure, vanity has driven both of us to do some borderline-silly things in this process. Jonathan flew home to Akron for fewer than twenty-four hours, just to have his teeth bleached by his dentist father. I had a series of seriously overpriced—and painful—facials in an attempt to forestall breakouts. Both of us want to look beautiful on our wedding day. But when it comes to our outer selves, it's not just about dressing up for the guests, or even for the pictures. It's about putting together the right items—totems, really—that will make us feel like bride and groom.

F WORDS OF WISDOM

Having things custom made is a good way to ease into the idea of being married and make it your own.

~

Most brides have one or two things that they get a little obsessive about. Don't feel bad! But choose your battles—you could drive yourself insane trying to get every little thing just so. Prioritize, and focus your attention on the elements of the wedding that mean the most to you. Then delegate (or at least don't micromanage) the rest.

~

Men often get the short end of the stick where wedding clothes are concerned, in part because they care less about them. How ironic that is, when you think about it: Women never wear their elaborate and expensive wedding outfits again, but men almost certainly could. It's a wonderful gesture to step in and make sure that your man is outfitted in a high-quality suit/tux/kilt/whatever that fits well and makes him look great. Consider making part of his outfit—tie, cufflinks, socks, shoes—your wedding gift to him, if you're adhering to that tradition.

~

Don't be afraid to take a big risk with something like a dress, suit, or a ring. If you've seen other things the designer/seamstress/tailor/jeweler has done, and you like them, chances are you won't be disappointed.

May 23

LETTING GO

Looking back at the wedding, from a rehearsal-dinner hangover, to a very convincing corpse pose, to the indelible, indisputable highlight.

IT'S THREE A.M. on the first night of our honeymoon, roughly three days after we said our vows, if you count the flight across the Atlantic. I'm sitting on the cool marble floor of a king-size bathroom at the fanciest hotel in Athens, trying to take deep breaths, sobbing into my notebook by the glow of a nightlight.

Determined not to wake Jonathan, I've picked my way through the pitch dark of our lavish suite, my hands out in front of me, feeling my way past the coffee table laden with flowers and chocolates, the walk-in closet, the champagne bucket on its stand, damp with condensation. What a metaphor. From the minute I said yes to his proposal, I was in unfamiliar territory, with a limited field of vision, not knowing what obstacles—and delights—were in front of me until I bumped up against them. Now I wonder: Will I regret writing this book? Or, more to the point, agreeing to publish it?

Momentary panic aside, these tears are more about release

than regret. The event that launched quite literally a hundred to-do lists is over. I've been using this notebook for writing and wedding planning alike, and, leafing back through the pages, there's a definite moment when my notes stop being reflective, and become very task oriented.

Our last week in New York and the week we spent in Nebraska before the wedding are an adrenaline and caffeine-fueled blur, a flurry of calls and e-mails, thank-you notes and strategy sessions. In an attempt to stop the madness, Jonathan and I decamped to the lodge on Thursday night, along with his parents and Brian. The goal was to have a quiet night at the wedding venue; time to center ourselves. It was quiet, all right, the lodge nearly empty, but I didn't feel centered. I felt like a marathoner who had just learned, at mile 26.1, that the finish line had been pushed back another eight hundred yards.

We did sneak in a dip in the pool, and a moment in the sauna, just the two of us, and, later, we had dinner with the rest of the Cohens. But mostly we worked. There were arrangements to make with the front desk and the catering coordinator, and then unmake when we changed our minds. There were lists of rehearsal-dinner guests to cross-reference, and goodie bags to fill for guests who would be staying overnight, a poem about Nebraska stapled to the front of each one. Finally, around eleven P.M., we started on the one big task I had been putting off: the seating chart. Three hours, countless iterations, and a couple bouts of screeching hysteria later, I was writing out the last of the kraft-paper place cards, each table's worth stamped with a different woodland animal, steadfastly refusing Jonathan's offers of help so the handwriting would match. I think I passed out with the Sharpie in my hand.

Friday had all the hallmarks of a dress-rehearsal day. For the moment, the work was done, and the anticipation was beginning to mount. Jonathan golfed, and I slept late, then greeted people as they arrived, including my poor family, pulling in like a pack-mule caravan, laden with items from home. I had lunch on the patio with my bridesmaids, and gave them their gifts: earrings I had commissioned from my jewelry-maker friend Ella. There was a quick rehearsal in the barn at five P.M., Jonathan and me wielding clipboards and presiding over the crowd, and then we, the wedding party, and those guests who despite weather and scheduling and the wretched airlines had managed to make it to the middle of the prairie in time, boarded buses and went rattling through the countryside back to Lincoln for a rehearsal dinner at the state capitol (a.k.a. my father's office building). It was a venue we'd more or less bullied the Cohens into using, and one everyone was really nervous about. It could have been too hot, too cold, too windy, too dark.

But you know what? Miracle of miracles, it was nearly perfect. The weather was magnificent, the food was excellent, and the tour of the building, heartfelt toasts, and general mood of the hundred-plus guests were great, great, and great.

So, unfortunately, was the open bar. I always, always drink too much at my own parties, and that night, though Lynn and Marvin were technically the ones throwing the dinner, I was in hostess overdrive. After another bumpy bus ride back to the lodge, its lounge packed with more, later-arriving friends, and one more monster round of hugs and kisses and toasts, all of a sudden it was Saturday morning.

And things were not all right.

I couldn't move. My mind was racing. I didn't want to see, or talk to, anyone but Jonathan, but we had planned to not see each other on the wedding day, until the big moment, and so he was out running around with his groomsmen.

Yes, I had a hangover on my wedding day. But I've had hangovers before. And usually, after an internal pep talk and a hot bath, all is more or less right again. But on the morning of my wedding, the old tricks didn't work.

It wasn't cold feet, in the traditional sense. All I wanted was to be holed up somewhere with Jonathan, away from this mess I had created. What I was experiencing, for the first time in my life, was a serious case of stage fright. For most of the morning, I was positive there was no way that I could walk down that aisle, stand up there, and say those words, with nearly two hundred people watching me.

Suddenly the task in front of me felt monumental, and weirdly separate from all the work and thinking I'd been doing for the previous year, both on the wedding and on the nuts and bolts of actually being married. What had I been doing with my time, if I'd failed to prepare myself for this? Even the smaller things that I had allowed myself to visualize weren't turning out anything like I'd imagined. For example, the yoga class that I had planned for the wedding party and other interested guests. When the instructor arrived, I was too weak and over-whelmed to actually participate. I felt I had to show up, of course, so I did, and I'm sure I looked alarming. We walked outside to set up for class on the sloping green lawn and faced a dull gray sky, studded here and there with more ominous clouds. While everyone else flowed through the poses, I just lay there in the grass and let the raindrops fall on my face. You could call it corpse pose, but I wasn't pretending.

Everyone went about their downward-dogging and planking and warrioring with nary a glance in my direction—probably obeying the unspoken rule that brides are allowed all kinds of bizarre behavior on their wedding day. And then, after the class, my mom said three magic words: "Get some sleep." So I went upstairs and took a nap. I was so out of it that it wasn't difficult to block out all the remaining tasks—setting up the flowers in the barn and the reception venue, putting out the cake—and hand them over to everyone else. I just completely let go.

When I woke up, I forced down a granola bar, then got out of bed, determined to make this second start to the day completely different from the first. With Jonathan's help, I got all the place cards set out, watched our DJ set up, and surveyed the reception room one last time.

> While everyone else flowed through the poses, I just lay there in the grass and let the raindrops fall on my face. You could call it corpse pose, but I wasn't pretending.

And with under three hours to go until the ceremony, I finally started getting ready. As I was having my hair piled on top of my head in one of the guest rooms, listening to my bridesmaid Sara's wacky stories, surrounded by the untouched bottles of vodka and cans of Red Bull that my brother had procured, the sun came out. Literally. It came streaming through the windows, suffusing everything with a golden glow. And the next thing I knew, I was dressed and made up and getting ready to walk toward the barn, surrounded by most of my favorite people in the whole wide world.

The ceremony itself is a disjointed collage, radiating out from an image of Jonathan's face. His steady smile and his even steadier brown eyes. His thumb brushing back and forth over the top of my hand. The bright sunlight and electric green visible through the open sides of the barn; the muted, shadowy interior. People smiling, people crying, people trying not to cry. My trying not to cry, and failing. My glancing at my father's face, and failing even more. The ring (which turned out stunning, by the way) sliding onto my finger. Strains of Bach from the trumpet quintet. The bright colors of the bridesmaids' dresses, and all the gorgeous flowers—sweet peas in pinks and peaches for the girls, roses for the guys. Jonathan being awed that the tie I had helped him pick out matched his boutonniere *perfectly*. And my bouquet, now drying on our kitchen counter back in New York, looking exactly like a childhood wish I didn't remember having.

With every visual memory of our wedding day, little corollary facts pop up, too, the back-story on how this or that thing came to be. When I think of the flowers, I think of our first, flaky florist, who could be a book unto himself, and the many borderline-ridiculous conversations with the one we eventually used. (Twenty-five dollars a stem for lilies of the valley? No thanks.) When I think of my college-age cousins playing the guitar and singing, I think of them as babies, then kids playing in the backyard. When I think of the ceremony itself, I think of Jonathan and me sitting on our raggedy old couch, parsing it out. I'm proud of how egalitarian and symmetrical it turned out to be. Both of us walked down the aisle with both parents. Each of us had a best man. And at the end, "You may kiss your spouse."

After the ceremony, I was overwhelmed by the torrent of love and praise—people even asked us if we had paid the birds to sing on cue. Turns out we assembled one amazing group of guests. I'd been obsessing for months about "wedding chemistry," about how some events just gel and others don't. Thankfully, our crowd took on a robust, unstoppable life of its own. The fact that everyone took so much delight in the surroundings and in each other underscores how very, very lucky we are to have these people in our lives. The one missing element was Abba and Mom Rosie. They can't travel, and so had celebrated at home, having, as I later learned, a candlelit dinner for two, complete with corsage and boutonniere. I had been reluctant to hire a videographer, sure it was unnecessary fuss and expense, but every time he passed by with his camera, I knew we were recording a message for them, and felt a bittersweet pang.

The DJ, our friend Adam, whom we flew in especially for the occasion, outdid himself. The dance floor was a crowd-surfing, sweat-soaked mess, and everyone was scheming about how to keep the bar open later. In a true party spirit, an older guest offered Jonathan a Viagra, just in case. People ate every last bit of the food—fried chicken and carved tenderloin sandwiches; potato salad and deviled eggs; veggies and salad—and had seconds of the gorgeous cake that my mom's friend Mara had lovingly baked and decorated. Jonathan and I walked around the room chatting and hugging, and I felt one thousand percent better than I had that morning, elated if not relaxed. I think I had a lettuce leaf or two, one deviled egg, and a couple of bites of cake. I drank lots of water, and carefully avoided the bar.

Several weeks before the wedding, I had pondered whether or not I should speak at the reception. I honestly can't remember attending a wedding where the bride spoke, but it seemed to me that making a statement of some kind was pretty important. You have your vows, sure, but that's ceremony. Why be voiceless on a day when you're the center of attention? So I was all fired up to write a brief speech. But, like so many things, that task fell by the wayside. I did wind up saying a little something, and so did Jonathan, but it was more process-oriented than anything else. *Thank-you-for-coming-that-way-to-the-bar-let's-eat!*

It's funny to look back at all the things we planned to do but abandoned along the way: the customized umbrellas in case of rain, the stick-on decorative vinyl letters to spell out our names and the date on the wall of the reception room, matching shawls for the bridesmaids, a signature wedding cocktail. The dance lessons may be the biggest-ticket item we abandoned. (We intended to go, and even took one lesson, but the place was alarming: blond Russian women, cash only, paid by the hour, in an anonymous, gray space with fluorescent lighting, fake plants, and a long, suspicious hallway.)

But we never planned to have a first dance, anyway, and so our moves weren't under the microscope. *Nothing* was as closely examined as I'd imagined it might be. I'm positive that none of the guests noticed anything "missing," or noticed any of the little snafus I recorded—just to get them on paper, and off my mind—in my notebook on the flight to Athens.

This is a long way of saying that, ultimately, our wedding wasn't exactly how I had envisioned it. I fully admit that I planned and worried and thought the day out to a ridiculous degree. But it turns out that all my efforts really did was set our wedding on a course, and then it took on a life of its own. It was different than I ever could have imagined, in more ways than I can count. And, ultimately, much, much better than I could have hoped.

I'm thankful that I didn't expect my wedding day to be the best day of my life, or even the happiest. It was, truly, the most up and down—or, rather, down and up—day I've lived to date. It was a topsy-turvy microcosm of one extraordinary year.

And here's the highlight: When we said our vows, and kissed, then kissed again, and walked out of the cool barn out into the dazzling sunlight, I was so present in that moment, so alive in my skin. The memory is indelible: I felt staggering joy, mixed with a sweet, sweet relief.

Since then, I've felt pretty numb to my surroundings, as if there's a soft, thick blanket between me and the rest of the world. It's exhaustion, I think, more than anything. But occasionally that same combination of joy and relief surges up, and washes over me in a powerful wave. One such wave hit me tonight, blasting me out of a fitful sleep. That's why I'm here on the bathroom floor in Athens—with a decadent honeymoon ahead of me—crying about what's behind me. It's a miracle that it's over. It's devastating that it's over. Finally, I'm finished with the F word. Tomorrow, we're off to the Greek Islands, as husband and wife.

A Fiancée's Reading List

Here are a few books that enlightened me, entertained me, or both while I was engaged, and writing about it.

Why We Love: The Nature and Chemistry of Romantic Love, Helen Fisher.
Fascinating. Gives a scientific and evolutionary basis for why we act the way we do.

The Year of Magical Thinking, Joan Didion
Gut-wrenching and beautifully written.

The Glass Castle, Jeannette Walls
Makes your family problems seem miniscule. A fascinating portrait of a very unconventional marriage, and family.

Emotionally Engaged: A Bride's Guide to Surviving the "Happiest" Time of Her Life, Allison Moir-Smith
A lifesaver. Helps you put all your crazy engagement emotions in context, and shows why it's vital to embrace them, rather than trying to shut them off.

The Conscious Bride: Women Unveil Their True Feelings About Getting Hitched, Sheryl Paul
The tone is a little new-agey, but the information in it is very good.

Between Two Worlds: The Inner Lives of Children of Divorce, Elizabeth Marquardt
Eye-opening.

The Other Boleyn Girl, Philippa Gregory
The perfect novel to read while planning a wedding. It's delicious—and it makes you feel very lucky to be marrying for love.

Wedding Zen: Calming Wisdom for the Bride, Susan Elia Macneal
A little trinket that I got as a gift—a fun read that reminded me to breathe.

Henderson's House Rules: The Official Guide to Replacing the Toilet Paper and Other Domestic Topics of Great Dispute, E. L. Henderson and David E. O'Connor
A helpful authority.

Here Comes the Bride: Women, Weddings, and the Marriage Mystique, Jaclyn Geller
A glorious rant. I bought and read this years ago, when I first began to suspect that women were a little too in love with weddings, and I've referred to it often over the past year.

Brides, Inc.: American Weddings and the Business of Tradition,
Vicki Howard
I interviewed Howard for a *Tango* article about wedding rings.
Her scholarship is impressive. There's a lot of stuff in here that
will really surprise you.

*I Do But I Don't: Walking Down the Aisle without Losing Your
Mind*, Kamy Wicoff
A very thoughtful memoir/advice tome. Sort of like this book,
only with more of a scholarly angle, and written in retrospect.

Oh, and the cohabitation study I cite in "Something in the Way
She Moves" is: S. M. Stanley, S. W. Whitton, and H. J. Mark-
man, "Maybe I Do: Interpersonal Commitment and Premarital
or Nonmarital Cohabitation." *Journal of Family Issues* 25(2004):
496–519. There also was a great article on the topic in the
July/August 2005 issue of *Psychology Today*. It's available on
www.psychologytoday.com: "The Perils of Playing House" by
Nancy Wartik.

Acknowledgments

M Y THANKS GO OUT to Danielle Chiotti, for seeing the book inside the melodrama; Elise O'Shaughnessy, for being brilliant, tireless, and almost always right; Diane Sollee, for selling me on marriage education and giving sound advice; Jason Schulte and everyone at office design for creating a stunning cover; Marnie Hanel and Savannah Ashour and the rest of the *Tango* team for convincingly feigning interest in the details of my wedding planning; Nancy and Larry Bare, for their unswerving support, even around blind corners; Marvin Cohen, for loving his son (and the rest of his family) enough to sit me down and grill me about what exactly I thought I was doing by writing this book, and for loving me enough to give me his blessing, anyway; Lynn Cohen, for treating me like a daughter from the word go; all my beautiful bridesmaids (Katie Finch, Allison French, Joanne Hsieh, Joyce Macek, Meredith McDonough, Mary Morrison, and Sara Otepka) for keeping me sane, and in stitches; Brad Bare, Brian Cohen, and Lauren Larsen, for their varsity-level cheerleading; and, of course, to Jonathan Cohen, whose optimism and faith got us here, for trusting me, and for delighting me every single day. I love you.